D0971602

The Fearless
Executive

The Fearless Executive

*Finding the Courage to
Trust Your Talents and
Be the Leader
You Are Meant to Be*

Alan Downs

AMACOM

American Management Association

New York • Atlanta • Boston • Chicago • Kansas City • San Francisco • Washington, D. C.
Brussels • Mexico City • Tokyo • Toronto

Special discounts on bulk quantities of AMACOM books are available to corporations, professional associations, and other organizations. For details, contact Special Sales Department, AMACOM, a division of American Management Association, 1601 Broadway, New York, NY 10019.
Tel.: 212-903-8316   Fax: 212-903-8083
Web site: www.amanet.org

This publication is designed to provide accurate and authoritative information in regard to the subject matter covered. It is sold with the understanding that the publisher is not engaged in rendering legal, accounting, or other professional service. If legal advice or other expert assistance is required, the services of a competent professional person should be sought.

The CIP data is available through the Cataloging-in-Publication division of the Library of Congress.

Printing number

10   9   8   7   6   5   4   3   2   1

In memory
of
Horace Moody Downs
whose life taught us
there is nothing to fear.

Contents

Preface   ix

ONE   Ignite Your Passion, Follow Your Talent   1

PART ONE   BREAKING THE CYCLE OF FEAR

TWO   Fear Chokes Your Talent   9

     Fear Susceptibility Inventory   26

THREE   Fear of Inadequacy: What If I Fail?   33

FOUR   Fear of Rejection: What If I Don't Make It to the Inner Circle?   48

FIVE   Fear of Scarcity: What If Someone Else Steals My Piece of the Action?   67

SIX   Fear of Reality: Isn't There a Quick Fix?   79

SEVEN   Fear of the Unknown: What Is Lurking Out There?   90

EIGHT   Fear of Authority: What If I Break the Rules?   100

NINE   Fear of Aging: What If I'm Obsolete?   108

PART TWO   TALENT: YOUR STRONGEST SUIT

TEN   Talent Is the DNA of Your Destiny   117

ELEVEN   Discovering Your Talent   125

TWELVE   Stop Trying to Fix Yourself   134

PART THREE   POSSESSED BY PASSION

THIRTEEN   What's a Nice Kid Like You Doing in a
              Joint Like This?   145

FOURTEEN   Remind Me, What Does Passion Look
              Like?   156

FIFTEEN   What Color Is Your Passion?   164

PART FOUR   ACTION IS THE ANTIDOTE TO FEAR

SIXTEEN   How to Get Lucky   173

SEVENTEEN   What's Stopping You?   179

PART FIVE   FORGED IN THE FIRE: THE PASSAGES OF A
             FEARLESS EXECUTIVE

EIGHTEEN   Passage One: Every Executive Starts in the
              Mailroom   185

NINETEEN   Passage Two: Proving Ground   189

TWENTY   Passage Three: The Fearless Executive   196

Index   209

Preface

In 1992 I was a human resources executive with one of the premiere retailing companies in the country, Dayton Hudson. Some years before that I earned a Ph.D. in organizational psychology and paid my dues working up the corporate ladder at Hewlett-Packard. I was earning a six-figure salary, living on a hillside in San Francisco, and spending every weekend at a lovely home in the Napa Valley.

There was only one problem. I was completely dissatisfied with my job. I did it well, but for me it was drudgery. Corporate layoffs were very fashionable in the early 1990s, and since I was trained as a psychologist, conducting layoffs was usually relegated to me. Month after month I spent canning hundreds of employees, all the while trying to convince myself and the managers who reported to me that we were doing the right thing. But deep inside I knew that many of the layoffs had been avoidable and were creating unnecessary havoc for the employees and the company.

One day (I can't remember exactly when it was, but I distinctly remember it happening), I walked into the office and knew I couldn't keep doing the same thing. It was as if somehow my soul had made the decision to quit that job. I didn't have a clue what else I would do; I just knew I couldn't keep doing what I had been doing. If I continued I would cross the line of no return: my life would be sold off, and my passions, now thoroughly repressed, would wither away for good.

So I quit. I had nothing more than a half-promise of a consulting job with my former employer, Hewlett-Packard, and I had a bit of money saved for living expenses. Still, I figured the worst that could happen was that the consulting work would dry up, and then I would go back to work for another employer before the money ran out. After all, Silicon Valley was booming, and just about anyone who wanted a job could get one. What I *really* wanted to do was consult and write, and that's where I was headed.

My boss and coworkers were shocked by my resignation. Did I have another job? No? Well, what was I going to do? Not sure? You should have seen the horrified looks on their faces.

Looking back on the decision to quit, I realize I could have been smarter about it and done a little planning. It certainly would have made life easier for me, and I won't recommend that you do what I did. At the time it seemed to me to be the only way I could straighten out my career and start following my passion. It never occurred to me (or to the authors of any of the many books I read on the subject) that it was entirely possible to "follow my bliss" inside the corporate walls.

I can't tell you what joy swelled within me after I made the decision to rediscover my passion. For the first time in a long time I began to feel something stirring inside me. A world of possibilities was opening up, and I was standing at the brink of a new life.

As I look back now I realize that the brink quickly became a precipice with a sharp drop-off. Sure, I was able to land a few more consulting jobs, but I was completely unprepared for managing a private consulting practice. There was so much to learn—and even more at stake.

Despite my inner turmoil, one thing was clear to me: I was really content sitting at my keyboard, pounding out an article or story (something I had begun doing to market my consulting services). I submitted my writing to magazines and periodicals, published only a few, and could have wallpapered my house with rejection slips. Little did I know that I was beginning a journey that would be as fulfilling as any I could imagine.

A year after quitting my corporate job I discovered I could make a pretty good living from publishing articles and management consulting. I also discovered I could do these things and live virtually anywhere as long as I had access to a computer, a fax machine, and an airport. I had a great offer for consulting work in New Orleans, so why not do it? Feeling my newly found freedom, I started out (once again) without much of a plan, but had a clear, gut feeling that New Orleans was the right place for me.

When I arrived in New Orleans I rented a small shotgun house in the Uptown section (not too far from the grand St. Charles Avenue) and found an office in the middle of the French Quarter. Every morning at about eight I would drive by the graceful mansions in the Garden District and through the Quarter to my office. Along the way, I would pass all of the other executives hurrying to their jobs in the business district and wonder if they loved what they did as much as I loved what I did.

Shortly after moving to New Orleans, I got a call from Steve Piersanti, publisher of Berrett Koehler Books in San Francisco, to whom I had sent a book idea. As it turned out, Steve wasn't terribly interested in my book idea but thought one of my articles, "Tale of a Reformed Corporate Executioner," would make a great book. Would I consider writing *that* book?

That was all the encouragement I needed. Within months I had put together a book proposal detailing my experience as a "corporate executioner"—the one person inside a company who planned and coordinated mass layoffs. As it turned out, Steve had given me great advice and several publishers were very interested in publishing my book. I was truly amazed at what was happening and ecstatic at the thought of becoming a real author. In hardly any time the book was accepted for publication by the American Management Association (AMACOM Books) and I was on my way to becoming a published author.

Publishing my first book filled me with great anxiety. I knew that what I was saying in the book might not sit well with many executives. I tried to push aside my worries, but they kept coming back. Even though I loved my newfound freedom, maybe this book would burn some bridges? Perhaps I would never consult again. I worried that companies would be terrified, if not angry, that I had been so bold with my criticisms.

When the book came out, the news media loved it. Almost every newspaper across the country carried something about the "repentant corporate executioner." *Good Morning America, NBC Nightly News, Wall Street Journal,* and *The New*

York Times all quoted my accusations for every CEO in the land to read. Even though I stood solidly behind what I had written, privately I was trembling at what I had done to my career.

What I didn't know at the time was that there was great wisdom in following my passion. Even though I never planned it, many senior executives supported my sharp criticism of certain inefficient and inhumane corporate practices, and my books gave them the courage (and the data) to speak out. I created a loyal following, and my consulting business increased.

In the years since that first book I have learned to trust the wisdom of my talent and passion. I love writing, and I love helping people to become successful at work and life. As a writer and a management psychologist I can do both; when I do, I find that my life is immensely satisfying, more than I ever thought possible. In my own awkward way I stumbled upon my calling and found the life I had always wanted.

So this is how I discovered the advice I now offer you within this book. I didn't learn it in graduate school or at a seminar. I *stumbled* upon it. Since I learned these lessons, I've used them to help many others rediscover their passion and find the life that brings them meaning and fulfillment.

In my executive seminar, *A Passion for the Top*, I've had the pleasure of watching many frustrated executives suddenly come alive. No one ever told them that what makes an executive successful is *a clear, unfaltering focus on whatever talent he or she has*. It isn't that you need a specific talent you don't have to be great at business—you simply need to learn how to trust your talent and follow your passion. That's all there is to it.

Learn from my experience: You don't have to leave your corporate job to follow your passion. In fact, what I learned from abruptly exiting my corporate job has helped many executives to discover success *within their corporate jobs*. The corporate job isn't the problem—it is a lack of focus on your talent. Once you get back on track with your talent and passion, you will transform your current job and every job after it into an outrageous success.

You can reignite your passion and become a fearlessly successful executive. Turn the page and let the adventure of your career begin.

ONE

Ignite Your Passion, Follow Your Talent

There are only three things you need to reach your highest potential in business:

Trust your talents. Follow your passion. Silence the fear.

And that is the whole truth about executive success.

How do I know? I'm a management psychologist who has worked for years in the field of selecting executives for high-level promotions. I've seen executives whose talents were rather limited, but who exploited them completely rise to become the heads of Fortune 100 companies. I've also seen some of the most gifted of executives fail simply because they failed to do the same.

Think of it this way: Piloting your successful executive career is much like landing an aircraft, where only three factors matter: altitude, distance, and wind resistance. In order to land the plane, the pilot must consistently find the ideal intersection of those three numbers. So you must strive for the goal of maximizing both your talent and passion while minimizing the resistance of fear. Nothing else in your executive career matters.

> Talent, hard work and unshakable commitment to your goals will serve you well.[1]
>
> Bernard W. Reznicek, CEO, Boston Edison

Your Only Strategic Advantage

Talent is your strategic advantage—your secret tool that gives you an edge over the competition. Passion is the motive—it's what propels you forward and gives you the strength to persist. Fear is the internal chain that holds you back from achieving your highest potential. How you handle these three things will determine the success of your executive career.

And here's the best-kept secret of executive success: *You've already got the talent and the passion to succeed.* What? That's right, you have "the right stuff." Executive success is not about having a particular kind of talent or passion—it's about *knowing* what your talent is and then exploiting it to the fullest. It isn't about being born with some special gift for managing or graduating from some sophisticated business school. *True executive success comes from knowing what you do best and doing only that.*

"Now really," you might say. "If it were that simple, wouldn't everyone be successful?" You make a good point. The only thing simple about it are the words—doing it is quite another story. The truth is that most of us don't really know what our talents are, much less exploit them to the fullest. We know what we are expected to do, but do we really know what we do best? More to the point, do we relentlessly focus ourselves on practicing that talent?

> The energy I sought, then and now, was the energy that comes from focusing all your powers, like a beam, on a single point.[2]
>
> John H. Johnson, Founder & CEO,
> Johnson Publishing Company
> (International publisher of *Ebony* magazine)

Not only are most of us unclear on our passion, but we believe the pursuit of passion to be somewhat foolish and irrelevant in business. Sure, we mouth the words about vision and passion, but when the rubber meets the road, we are more concerned about doing what we think will "get us ahead in the game" than doing what we truly love to do.

Take Bob, for example. Bob is an electrical power engineer who truly loves designing electrical systems. He works for a large public utility company that provides electrical power to much of southern Florida. For years, Bob worked in the engineering design department as a design engineer, creating the power grids for new subdivisions being built on land reclaimed from the Everglades. After ten years or so, Bob discovered that he had reached the top of his pay scale in the design department and that the only way he could increase his salary and job title was to accept a position on the company's executive track. Taking that job meant that Bob had to leave the design department and begin a five-year rotation that would move him through all the basic functions of the company. His first assignment was that of human resource director for a division. Later, he rotated through public relations. None of these jobs were particularly appealing to Bob, nor did they use his design talents. They did, however, increase his position and salary.

After several years of rotation, Bob landed in the position of managing one of the company's older fossil fuel plants. The plant had been plagued with problems for many years and Bob had been chosen as the executive to run it. It was known to be the "old dog" of the company's power plants. For Bob, it was a boring and unrewarding job, but it was what he felt he had to do to get ahead.

About the same time that Bob had begun the executive track program, a friend of his who had also worked in the design engineering department had left the company. He went to work for a smaller firm that designed power grids and private generation systems for companies that were seeking to lower their expenses by generating their own power. Bob's friend excelled at what he did and before long he was a partner in the firm, making more money than he ever could have working for the utility design department. The best part was that he never had to give up what he loved doing. Two years after Bob took the job managing the fossil fuel plant, his friend hired him away to work for his design firm. Finally, Bob was back in the environment where he thrived, both personally and professionally.

What would have happened if Bob had never abandoned his talent and passion for designing electrical systems? We'll never know. One thing is certain: When Bob focused on what he thought would get him ahead, he slowly moved his career off track by taking a job that was no longer using the strategic advantage of his talent.

Executive success is so simple, yet so difficult. The temptation to abandon your talent and passion, to do a job that doesn't tap your strengths and isn't something you enjoy, is all around. It's so easy to get caught up in the race to the top, and adopt a win-at-all-costs philosophy.

CHAMPIONS OF BUSINESS

Think about some of the great executives of our time:

Jack Welch (General Electric)
Bill Gates (Microsoft)
Warren Buffet (Berkshire Hathaway)
Richard Branson (Virgin Atlantic)
Lew Platt (Hewlett-Packard)

What each of these outrageously successful executives shares is that they exploit their talent and are deeply in love with what they do. They are not necessarily the most talented, the brightest, or the best educated. Instead, they hold a vigilant focus on exploiting their strengths and doing what they love.

What's equally important about all of these executives' careers is that when their talents were not valuable to an organization, they didn't try to change their talents (even if they could); instead, they changed the *situation* so that their talents were fully utilized. For you that may mean restructuring a job, moving within the organization, or even moving to another organization. To remain without change would require you to trade off yourself to please the organization; while that might please your superiors in the short run, it will only diminish your executive potential and hurt your career. You will never truly excel at something that isn't within your talents.

FEAR: THE DARK ADVISER

So why is trusting your talent so difficult? Simply, you are betrayed by your fear. This fear tells you that you are inadequate, that you must be something other than what you are. It tells you that you need something for success that you don't have. It tells you that you don't have the right degree, the right look, the right skills, or the right experience. It tells you that if you pursue your innate talents, you will utterly fail. Instead, it demands that you live according to others' expectations and stay in jobs that don't mine your talents, because you *must* keep earning the big salary.

These fears are not about legitimate danger. Whereas it is rational and healthy to avoid real danger, this angst is an obsession with imagined calamity. It is a generalized, ambiguous feeling of impending demise that influences you.

- "They might not approve of me." (*They* are never as ominous or omnipotent as we imagine *them* to be).
- "I won't be able to work in my field again." (This rarely, if ever, happens.)
- And the worst of all: "I will fail." (Failure is an experience everyone must taste from time to time—it is, by no means, the horrible experience we often dread.)

Ironically, when you listen to these fears and allow them to control your behavior, they influence you to create the very thing you are trying to avoid! When you fear rejection, you behave in patronizing, perhaps even in cloying ways that others find offensive. When you fear failure, you lose your confidence and perform less capably.

Another startling and destructive by-product of fear is that it not only blocks you from developing your talents, it can prevent you from discovering your talents in the first place. It binds you to the safe and familiar path, preventing you from experimenting with your abilities and discovering the possibilities of what you are capable. Fear tells you:

"Why should I tell the CEO my ideas? I've never put together a corporate strategy."
"Why should I volunteer for the reorganization committee? I don't know anything about human resources."
"Why should I write the proposal? I've never done that before."

Fear blocks you from exploring and experimenting, and keeps you from discovering your true talents. Not until you silence these strong voices of fear are you able to experience your fullest potential and come to know your capabilities, and thus achieve your greatest success.

Fear asks you to trade off the power of your talents to become something that appears to be better, only to become a counterfeit of yourself. It is a vicious cycle that robs your potential and, ultimately, your success.

Confronting fear is something every successful executive must go through. Before you can embrace your talents fully, you must meet those fears face-to-face. It is a required right of passage. Unless you uncloak the dark advisers and expose them for what they are—nothing more than imagined devils—they will continue dogging you.

Throughout this book, we will explore how you can apply these basic principles and achieve your highest executive potential:

Trust your talent. Follow your passion. Silence the fear.

The next section of this book takes a close look at the voices of fear that can cause you to derail your executive career before it ever really takes off.

NOTES

1. Michael Ames, *Pathways to Success* (San Francisco: Berrett Koehler Books, 1994).
2. John Johnson, *Succeeding against the Odds* (Amistad Press, Inc., 1989).

PART ONE

BREAKING THE CYCLE OF FEAR

TWO

Fear Chokes Your Talent

> Many men are so amazed and astonished with fear, they know not where they are, what they say, what they do . . . and it makes their hearts ache, sad and heavy. They live in fear, are never free, resolute, secure, never merry, but in continual pain. Fear makes our imagination conceive what it lists, invites the devil to come to us . . . and tyrannizeth over our phantasy more than all other afflictions.[1]
>
> Robert Burton, 1577–1640,
> English clergyman and scholar

So what is it that keeps you from completely trusting your talents? Fear. Fear is the voice that whispers in your ear and keeps you doubting your ability to be successful. "I wouldn't do that if I were you," it seems to say. "Better stay with something that is more secure." The messages of fear are quietly cunning, and unless you learn to recognize them, you are susceptible to their influence.

THE DARK ADVISER

When I think about how fear betrays us, I think of how the infamous Rasputin betrayed the Russian monarchy shortly after the turn of the century. Rasputin was born as a peasant in Siberia. By the age of thirty, he had left his family to become a wandering holy man. With little education and a seductive demeanor, Rasputin quickly gained a reputation for faith healing and debauched behavior. During a visit to St. Petersburg in 1905, Rasputin was presented at the court of Empress Alexandra, where he was able to relieve the suffering of her hemophiliac son and heir to the Russian throne. Enamored with Rasputin's supposed magical powers, Empress Alexandra made him a regular member of her entourage. When Emperor Nicholas II left St. Petersburg for the front lines of the Russian army during World War I, Rasputin wielded tremendous power over the Empress and, consequently, over Russian politics. Under Rasputin's sway, she appointed many of his incompetent cronies to high government positions. In matters of both internal and foreign affairs, she sought and implemented his advice. Many historians believe it was the Empress's acceptance of Rasputin's self-serving and flawed advice that ultimately caused the Czarist monarchy to fall.

Fear influences the executive much as Rasputin did the Empress. It lurks in the background and constantly whispers misguided advice. It seems to be speaking on behalf of your own good but, in reality, betrays your confidence. It entices you to abandon your rational faculties, and adopt other, fear-based decisions. If you allow it full reign, fear will eventually precipitate the demise of your career.

Here's the crux of the matter: *The executive seeking his or her highest potential must learn to distinguish between the voices of fear and the true dangers of reality.* The only way to do that is to recognize the irrational voices of fear.

Rasputin met his fate when a group of Russian aristocrats confronted him during a midnight tea party and assassinated him. So it is with fear; you must uncover its subversive influence and thus eliminate its control over your life.

It's More Than a Reaction—It's an Attitude

There are two kinds of fear. There is the *state* of fear and the *trait* of fear. The difference is very simple, but important to understand. A *state* of fear is what you feel when you encounter something that is unexpected and potentially harmful. Perhaps you feel this kind of fear when you walk down a dark alley at night or when you barely avoid having a traffic accident. Those feelings are an immediate reaction to danger that is in the present.

A *trait* of fear, however, is something very different. It is an enduring attitude of fear. You are experiencing a trait of fear when you resist taking financial risks or when you avoid unfamiliar social interactions. The trait of fear is not connected to any *present* danger; it is about an *imagined* danger. You imagine that taking risks might hurt your financial standing or that a particular social interaction will be embarrassingly awkward. You have not encountered either of these situations when you feel the trait of fear—they are strictly imagined.

As a rule of thumb, a state of fear happens when *you experience danger, then you feel fear.* On the other hand, a trait of fear is when you *feel fear and avoid action altogether.* Of the two, the trait of fear has a far greater influence over your life and career. Throughout this book, it is the trait of fear that we discuss.

The *trait* of fear is enduring and has a greater potential to damage your executive career. It is a long-term attitude of fear that begins with an unhealed wound but that with time has grown large and independent, no longer connected to the event that caused it. It lingers in your mind, coloring your thoughts and prompting your behavior. This trait of fear is what steals your birthright—the talents and opportunities that are given to you throughout your life. It always diminishes you to the lowest common denominator.

The trait of fear is free floating and is no longer connected to any real danger. Rather than a healthy reaction to impending danger (as in a *state* of fear), the trait of fear clouds your thoughts and causes your actions to be overenergized and clumsy. In reality, fear creates more danger than it purports to avoid.

A trait of fear is a choice. Not an easy choice, but a choice all the same. Fear begins with a wound and, if you allow it, grows within your mind. Over time, fear begins to color your life and decisions, affecting all of your behavior. It can provoke you to the extremes of passivity or aggression and distort otherwise rational thinking. It rarely, if ever, inspires the best of decisions.

WHAT IS FEAR?

Let's roll up our sleeves and go to work on identifying just what is the influence of fear. To start, let's look at the nine basic properties of fear.

1. *Fear lives only in the mind.* At first glance, this may seem painfully obvious, but take a minute to seriously consider the fact that fear does not exist in your environment—it lives solely in your mind. Fear is something that you do to yourself. No one can make you afraid except you.

Even though you know that fear is a mental thing, when you are acting upon fear you often treat it as if it is something in your environment. It is as if your fear is created by what is happening to you: "I am afraid because ———— is happening." You convince yourself that fear is the only rational reaction to the situation, when, in fact, it is mostly irrational.

A discussion about fear wouldn't be complete without looking at the source of most fear: emotional wounding. This is uncomfortable to talk about, but crucial. One executive with whom I work likes to say that the topic of emotional wounds has a "high cringe factor." It seems just a little too personal to be discussed in a business setting. Nevertheless, if you really want to master fear, you've got to take a serious look at the emotional wounds, where the fear is rooted.

The Unhealed Wound

Life is full of opportunities for emotional wounding. In fact, there may be times in our lives when that's all we seem to experience. One of the true miracles of the human spirit, however, is that we contain within ourselves the power to heal our wounds. Ninety-nine percent of the time your body becomes ill, it heals itself. This is also true with your mental and emotional well-being—you contain the facility to heal your own wounds.

The key to a successful life and career lies not in how you are wounded (we are all wounded by our environment and by our own bad choices), but in how you choose to heal your wounds. Remarkably, you are at liberty to control the extent of your own healing. How you interpret your wounds has a great deal to do with how you heal. If you choose to make yourself a victim to the wound, then the wound grows larger and controls your life. If you choose to focus on all the potential of life that remains within you, the wound diminishes and loses its control.

A Real Superman

One of the great stories of triumphant healing comes from the Hollywood actor who brought Superman to life on the big screen: Christopher Reeve. After a tragic riding accident left his spine severed in 1995, he struggled through the recovery from an injury that left much of his body paralyzed. Today, he is quite active, refusing to allow his condition to control him. His accomplishments since the accident are truly remarkable:

▭ He has established a charitable foundation to raise awareness and money for research on spinal cord injuries.

▭ His work as director of the HBO film *In the Gloaming* earned him an Emmy nomination, one of five that the film received.

▭ His speeches at the 1996 Democratic National Convention and the Academy Awards inspired people around the country and the world.

▭ He has testified before Congress on behalf of health insurance legislation and lobbied for increased federal funding for spinal cord research.

Had he chosen, Reeve could have viewed his paralysis as reason to become withdrawn and bitter. At several critical points, he remembers, he could have completely given up and asked the doctors not to continue sustaining his life. But he chose not to give up, and instead has transcended the physical condition to reclaim his life and reach for his highest potential.

When some traumatic event occurs, like Christopher Reeve's accident, it pierces the outer layers of your being, wounding your emotions and sometimes even your body. The healing of that wound begins when you call upon the fierce power of your self-confidence. Sometimes that healing comes in the form of learning to live with a wound and to transcend it. Sometimes, healing removes that wound altogether.

When you do not adequately heal your wounds, you develop "scar tissue" around the wound. Emotional wounds that are not healed properly are particularly likely to become enduring trouble spots. When others—sometimes unknowingly—touch your old wounds, you lash out at them. You become defensive, angry, and fearful in the area of your wound.

This is where fear enters the picture. Whenever a situation appears to be similar to one that wounded you, you feel fear. The feeling is a lingering remnant of that old wound, reminding you of the pain you once felt. This brings us to another very important property of fear.

2. *Feeling fear is not the same thing as acting upon fear.* There is a huge difference between *feeling* fear and *acting* upon fear. Risky situations elicit fear from everyone. We've all had fearful experiences in life and certain events can call up within us that fear. Nobody, not even the most successful and courageous of executives, is immune to feeling fear.

Acting upon fear is a different story. The feeling of fear tells you to do one thing: escape danger. Most often in business, this means to stop and take no action. In other words, avoid the danger by not proceeding forward. Rather than take even the most intelligent risk, fear pushes you toward inactivity. It asks of you, "Why take the risk?" This brings me to another property of fear.

3. *Even the most successful executives feel fear.* No matter how much experience or success an executive may have, from time to time he or she feels fear. I can't tell you how many times this one statement would have helped me in my early career. I had watched senior executives walk into situations that were more dangerous than a pit of vipers and coolly handle them with strength and grace. I wondered, "How could they handle this without seemingly being afraid?"

When it came time for me to handle such situations (usually involving large groups of angry employees to be laid off), I was quite anxious, to say the least. I wondered, "How do other executives do this kind of thing without being afraid?" If only I had known then what I know now. *They're all feeling afraid*. They wouldn't be human if they weren't. Even the most successful CEOs feel fear when they are in potentially dangerous territory. What makes them successful is that they have learned the art of moving past the feeling and dealing with the reality, no matter how treacherous it may be.

The next time you feel like you're the only one who's nervous about giving the big presentation or giving bad news to the big boss, stop yourself. What you're feeling is what we all feel. The real question is how will you handle that feeling?

4. *Fear is about imagined catastrophes, not present danger.* Another distinct characteristic of fear is that it creates an irrational belief in imaginary catastrophes rather than causing an avoidance of true danger. In other words, fear is an ongoing feeling of dread and panic. In your mind you enlarge the possibility of injury far beyond reality, to the point where you convince yourself that something very dire will happen if you do not take evasive action.

You tell yourself:

> "Other people must like me, or I will be alone and unloved."
> "I must be successful, or I will be a failure."
> "I must please the boss, or I will lose my job."

You create an exaggerated dichotomy in your mind: The desired outcome is ALL good, while every other outcome is EXTREMELY bad. You tell yourself that the desired outcome must be achieved, and you must avoid other outcomes at all costs. Notice how in the above fear statements the imagined consequences have become generalized and enlarged: "I will be alone and unloved." "I will be a failure." "I will lose my job." Fear is no longer about avoiding real dangers; it is about avoiding *imaginary* catastrophes.

What If

Another characteristic of fear is that it feeds upon "what if" instead of "what is." At any point in life, the universe of what could happen is always larger than what is really happening.

There are an infinite number of possibilities, but only one present moment. Of all the things that could go wrong (or right), only one will happen. Fear begins to gain momentum when we give more of our attention to this surge of possibilities instead of to the present moment.

Conquering fear demands living in the present. Right now, what is happening? In this moment, what is the best I can do?

The epic movie *Titanic* gives a wonderful illustration of how staying clearly focused on the present can conquer the madness of fear. In the final half hour before the luxury liner turns vertically and slips into the water, the hero of the story, Jack, and his leading lady, Rose, struggle to escape the lower decks of the ship, which were filling quickly with water. As they encounter obstacle after obstacle in their struggle to stay above the water, Jack gives Rose clear, concise instructions that are focused on their present dilemma rather than upon the chilling possibilities of what might ultimately happen to them when the ship goes under. They focus on getting just one deck higher above the encroaching water. Once on the top deck, they focus on climbing to the end of the ship that is above the water. Then, they focus on clinging to the railing as it flips into the midnight air. Finally, they focus upon staying afloat after the ship has been completely submerged.

Clearly, Jack and Rose's situation was dire. But attending to the horrible possibilities of what lay ahead would have only fueled their panic, immobilizing them and diminishing their chances of survival even further. Instead, they locked into each situation as it presented itself.

Other passengers, consumed with fear, threw themselves off the upper decks to a certain death in the waters below. Their fear forced them to create the very situation they were desperate to avoid. Granted that the chances of survival for any of the remaining passengers were slim, they were even less for those who gave in to panic.

Likewise, many executives fail because they become obsessed with the "what if." For example, in the early 1980s many high-technology company executives became notorious for "analysis paralysis." Trying to succeed in an industry that was moving swiftly and somewhat erratically, these executives attempted to anticipate all the possibilities of the future before making any decisions. Since they were ultimately incapable of accurately predicting the future, they failed to act in the moment. Their fear, fueled by an obsession of "what if," prevented them from capitalizing upon the opportunities of the moment.

Much has changed in the management of high-technology companies. Today, successful managers focus on shrinking the time to market and building flexible organizations that can change quickly to accommodate the whims of the present market. In other words, far more energy is devoted to responding to present challenges than to anticipating all the possible changes that may occur in the future.

5. *Fear is a breach of trust in yourself.* Not only does fear cause you to imagine dire traumas, *it keeps you continually doubting your ability to prevent or avoid these traumas.* In other words, when you engage in fear you lose faith in yourself and your abilities. It is a very destructive and irrational mind game you play on yourself. Ironically, fear actually *causes* you to become the helpless creature you have imagined yourself to be.

The irrational beliefs of fear are a particular problem for the business executive. After all, business is all about results. We work in order to produce a product or service; these outcomes define the very nature of business. When the executive engages in fear, he imagines many cataclysmic outcomes and loses faith in his ability to avoid these disasters. As a result, his decision-making ability is severely hampered. He makes low-risk decisions and then continues to mettle with the issue far more than is necessary. In the end, his obsessive tinkering may actually create the disaster he is trying to avoid.

In this way, fear begets more fear. When an executive fears that a project will fail, it often does, causing him to be even more fearful the next time the same situation arises. Unchecked fear feeds on more fear until it completely destroys that executive's career.

Fear is a breach of trust in your talents. Instead of knowing confidently that you have done your best (and that it is enough), you doubt that your best is sufficient. You lose faith in your internal guidance system. Through fear, you chisel a crack in the wall of your self-confidence and peace of mind.

The truth is, in any situation you can't control all circumstances. In fact, there is much in this world that is beyond your control. It is always possible that no matter how well you do a task, disaster could strike. Trusting yourself means that you know you have done everything you can possibly do to achieve the desired outcome. The clear answer to eliminating fear is to relinquish an outcome by trusting your talents. *You do your best and then let it go.* You set your eyes on a result and work to achieve it, but in the end you relinquish it, knowing that you have done all you can do *and that it is enough.* By trusting your best effort, you inoculate yourself against fear.

6. *Fear grows in the vacuum created by ignorance.* Ignorance is another factor that feeds fear. The lack of knowledge about a situation is sufficient to cause you to fear, without any real danger being present. In the Middle Ages, mental patients were thought to be possessed by demons and were thrown out of their villages and forced to roam the wilderness for food. The deep sea was once thought to be inhabited by monsters who destroyed ships at will. American Indians were once feared as uneducable savages.

Today, we know all of this to be folklore, not reason for fear. As we have explored other lands and cultures, we have learned things we did not know before, and that knowledge has helped quell many of our fears.

Nevertheless, fear-by-ignorance operates throughout modern corporations. Many executives hold a shaky understanding of accounting and fear many of the routine financial dealings, most notably budgeting. Others have no knowledge of the functions of the human resources department, and are suspicious of any inquiries from that department. Cross-functional territorialism, wherever it is found, is almost always based on fear-by-ignorance of departments other than one's own.

Secrecy, whether intentional or not, creates ignorance, which in turn fuels fear. No better example of this phenomenon exists than the assassination of President John Kennedy. The events surrounding the killing of Kennedy and the subsequent investigations by the Warren Commission were all shrouded in tight secrecy, keeping the American public largely in the dark about the details of what actually occurred. That ignorance has fueled hundreds of fear-based books, conspiracy theories, and several major motion pictures blaming the Mafia, the FBI, the CIA, Cuban communists, and the U.S. Government. The secrecy surrounding the assassination augmented our fears about the numerous potential masterminds behind the assassination.

So it is in the corporation. For example, companies that insist on a closed-door process for promotions create enormous fear among those whose careers might be affected. When these executives are kept ignorant of the factors involved in such decisions, they begin guessing, fearful that every action they take may be used to assess their potential. And so it is with any number of other processes that are kept secret, such as salaries and bonuses, layoffs, budget allocations, or transfers. The list goes on and on.

Secrecy and ignorance are the antithesis of knowledge. Knowledge is indeed power: *The more we know, the less fuel there is for fear.*

7. *Fear is the opposite of growth.* Of course, there is no such thing as a "sure thing." Everything, no matter how regular or predictable, carries a risk. Modern physics has taught us that permanence is nothing more than a temporal illusion. Everything, at every moment, is in a state of flux. To believe that something is absolute and unchanging is to hold an illusion. To try and stop something from changing is to stop growing *and to start dying.*

Especially in business, risk is all around you everyday. If you are to be successful, you must befriend risk, understand it, and define its limits. How much are you willing to put on the line? What is acceptable risk?

Comfort with acceptable levels of risk is in direct contrast to the way in which many executives operate. Instead, they try to minimize all risks. Their goal is to make decisions that have little potential for failure. And just as is true in financial markets, the decisions with the lowest possible risk yield the lowest possible return. Since all growth requires risk, eliminating risk eliminates growth.

The executive who attempts to minimize all risks is doomed to mediocre performance, at best. This is the executive who won't make a proposal until he has watered it down with everyone's ideas. Further, he won't act until every possible player has agreed to his actions. Nothing radically new or innovative comes from this executive, for that carries far too much risk. He always stays on the safe path—one that, in reality, is the path of fear.

In a 1997 interview, Katharine Graham, publisher of the *Washington Post,* told of her early years at the helm of the newspaper. Thrust unexpectedly into the chief decision-maker role at the *Post* after her husband's suicide, she remembers how she tried to quell her fears by gaining everyone's approval for her decisions. She made the rounds with each decision, trying to win the blessing of all the major players at the newspaper. But those decisions, she remembers, were not the best of her career. Later on, after she conquered her fear, she would seek her staff's input, but when the time came, she made her own decision.[2]

8. *Fear feeds upon itself.* One of the properties of fear that makes it so difficult to overcome is that it feeds upon itself. When you are afraid and take action to alleviate fear, you feel a sense of relief. That sense of relief gives you the feeling that you have done the right thing, when all you have really done is alleviate your feeling of fear. So what are you likely to do the next time you are afraid? Immediately act to alleviate the fear so you can feel the relief.

During the height of a fearful experience, your sensory arousal and muscle tension increase. Your body, in response to this heightened state of awareness, begins to produce natural tranquilizers that will calm you and level your experience to a more normal state. Once the fear is alleviated, the biological processes that calmed you down actually cause you to swing past a normal state into a more relaxed mode (i.e., a strong sense of relief). Scientists have identified this as the opponent process model of fear, which is pictured in Figure 2-1. The dip into relief is what can make fear self-sustaining. How? The relief that follows fear provides a positive reward for the fear—even when the fear is irrational and unjustified. Thus, irrational fears can produce a positive result (i.e., a feeling of relief), which seems to justify the fear and increase the likelihood of the person acting on that fear in the future.

Figure 2-1. Opponent process model of fear.

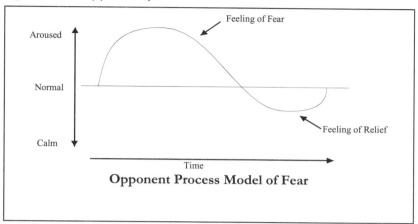

The same thing happens with executives. After escaping a fearful situation, they feel relief. Consequently, the next time that situation arises, they act upon their fear in order to feel relief. (Notice that the executive doesn't stick with the situation and solve it, but rather learns to act upon the fear.) It doesn't take too many of those experiences before the executive becomes convinced that acting out that particular fear is the correct thing to do.

The important point is that what brings the executive relief isn't solving the situation *but alleviating the fear.* In other words, the decision is driven by what will reduce the feeling of fear rather than what is the best decision in that situation. In this way, fear becomes a self-sustaining system of less than optimal executive decisions.

9. *Fear often attracts what it attempts to avoid.* Earlier in this chapter I mentioned that when we act upon fear we create the situation we actually fear. In other words, fear tends to attract what is feared.

As a kid growing up in the South, I started riding horses before I attended kindergarten. By the time I was in first grade, I was already riding in local rodeos. One of the memories I have of that time in my life was of being thrown off my horse right before entering the arena. My horse was a high-spirited Arabian mare, who was sometimes given to quick moves and rearing on her hind legs. After I was thrown, my dad, an experienced horseman, did something that on the surface seems harsh but was incredibly wise. He made me get back on the horse and keep riding. It was a terrifying experience for me, but it forced me to push through the fear. After a few hours of careful riding, my fear began to fade. Had I not gotten back on that horse, there is a very real possibility that my fear would have ruined horseback riding for me—and I would not have had a pastime that I have enjoyed my whole life.

The wisdom of getting back on the horse is something every successful executive must learn. You see, horses (like people) have an uncanny ability to sense fear; when they sense their rider is afraid, they often react with rough behavior. That, of course, only reinforces the rider's fear, causing the horse to continue misbehaving, and the cycle continues. By pushing through the fear, I was able to calm my fear and break this cycle. I was too young to know it at the time, but had I allowed my fear of the horse to grow by not getting back in the saddle, it would have grown, producing more riding accidents and more fear.

Many executives suffer from this same cycle of fear. They fear they will fail and they subsequently act in ways that cause them to fail. Likewise, they fear that they will be rejected, so they elicit rejection from their peers. It is a very real phenomenon and it is at the core of the destructive power of fear.

Overcome by Fear

Not all that long ago, I worked with an executive who destroyed her promising career in this very manner. Because my work requires a great deal of travel, I rarely have the opportunity to become involved with organizations in my local community. A few years ago, however, I reluctantly accepted the position of president of the board for a nonprofit organization that I felt was doing some great work. Shortly after joining the board of directors, the nonprofit agency hired a new executive director. The candidate who was hired was perfectly qualified on paper to do the job and had stood above all the other candidates produced by a national search. She had a great deal of experience, a good education, and was very engaging. Everyone involved in the organization felt she was perfect for the job.

Unfortunately, prior to taking her new job, Susan (not her real name) spoke extensively with a disgruntled former staff member. This person warned her about all the people who might "undermine" her, and all the possible ways that she could fail. Susan apparently internalized much of this information and started her new job with a deep suspicion that some of the staff would be working against her. Outwardly she was as accommodating and supportive as could be expected, although inwardly she kept a wary eye on those she thought might not support her.

Within months of her hire, staff members began to quit. The exodus didn't really alarm me, since this often happens when a new manager is installed in an organization. Each person who left had a different reason—one had a new job, another wanted to work from home—all the usual reasons why people leave. Six months after Susan's hire, however, the exodus was still continuing, and it was more than just staff members. Other agencies that worked closely with the organization began to refuse to participate in our programs, and local community leaders whose support was critical to our mission began to be less enthusiastic about our organization.

Nine months into Susan's tenure, I really became concerned. Here was an executive who seemed to be doing all the right things, and yet everything was slowly falling apart. Worst of all, donations were tapering off and we were headed into troubled financial waters. I began meeting regularly with Susan to discover what was happening, and over time a picture of fear began to emerge. Susan had come to this job fearing the worst, and slowly but surely she was creating what she feared.

When she and I talked about the staff members who had quit, she mentioned that she hadn't done much to encourage them, because "they didn't support her vision for the organization." When we discussed the lack of involvement with other agencies, she said that she suspected that a few of them had been trying to hire away our best staff members (and, in fact, they had hired one of our best fund-raisers), and consequently she had broken off those relationships. As for the decreased involvement with community leaders, she had some equally fearful excuse about why she had discouraged those relationships.

After her first year, I initiated a standard review of Susan's performance by asking all the board members to rate her job performance (something that is done for most executives during their first year). The results, which weren't stellar but not all that bad, were then given to Susan. Surprisingly, she resigned after receiving the feedback.

Needless to say, we were all shocked at her sudden departure. What we uncovered in the weeks that followed was that Susan had interpreted every ordinary conflict as an intentional attempt to "undermine" her leadership. In her mind, anything less than unquestioning and glowing support for her actions was an assault on her credibility.

I contacted former staff members and discovered that several had quit because Susan had constantly interfered with their jobs—second-guessing their decisions and overriding their conversations with our clients. When they had complained about this to her, she seemed to interfere even more. Finally, they had had enough, and quietly departed the organization. Apparently, Susan had interpreted their feedback to her as evidence that they truly weren't supporting her and she became even more vigilant of their work. When they quit the organization, she was relieved instead of being greatly concerned with the critical loss of talented staff. The final straw for Susan had been the board's evaluation of her performance, which only confirmed her growing fears. Not only was the staff against her, so was the board! All the board members agreed that it wasn't that at all—but through the lens of fear, it appeared that way to Susan. The bottom line was this: Susan's fear of rejection actually created the situation she most feared.

Perhaps Susan's story seems a bit on the paranoid side, but I encourage you to look at the executives with whom you work. More importantly, look closely at yourself and your own career. I think you'll find that many of us act exactly the way Susan did. We fear something, and consequently we attract the very thing we fear into our careers. Scientists have for years called this the "self-fulfilling prophecy." Whatever label we use, it is a powerful force that can derail your career.

Breaking the cycle of executive fear means that you deliberately stop acting out your fear. Even though you continue to feel it, you push through it. You get back up on the horse that threw you, put on your brave face, and keep pushing forward.

BREAKING THE CYCLE OF FEAR

Are you ready to make a positive change in your career? If you are willing, I can promise you will get extraordinary results, so let's get down to work. There are three distinct steps to breaking the cycle of fear that undermines your executive career. They are:

1. Acknowledge and confront the irrational beliefs that underlie the fear.
2. Make a conscious effort to push past the fear even though you continue to feel it.
3. Take positive action in the direction of your fear.

In the chapters that follow, we will take a close look at the common fears that can undermine your executive career, and how to implement these three steps to free your career from the influence of fear. Each chapter discusses a particular fear. At the end of each chapter is a section titled "Breaking the Cycle of Fear," in which we look at some very practical ways to implement these three steps and put yourself on the track to achieving your best.

NOTES

1. R. Burton, *The Anatomy of Melancholy* (New York: Oxford University Press, 1994).
2. Katherine Graham, interview by Terry Gross, *Fresh Air,* National Public Radio, February 17, 1997.

Fear Susceptibility Inventory

On the following pages, you will find a list of pairs of statements like the sample that follows. Read the two choices, and place a check mark in the white box beside the statement that is true for you. In some cases, both statements will be true, in which case you should select the one that is *most* true. Sometimes both statements will be less than true, in which case you should select the one that is the least *untrue*.

Selecting a statement does not mean that you agree fully with it—it only means that you think that statement is truer than the statement to which it is compared. Do not spend too much time on any one pair; go with your first impression.

Remember: No one else will see your results unless you allow them to see them. It is important to be completely honest in your responses.

Example:

Other people tend to think I am more talented than I really am.						
Early in any business relationship, it is important for me to show of what I am capable.	√					

FEAR SUSCEPTIBILITY INVENTORY

	A	B	C	D	E	F	G
Other people tend to think I am more talented than I really am.							
Early in any business relationship, it is important for me to show of what I am capable.							

	A	B	C	D	E	F	G
More often than not, it is a mistake for me to reveal my weaknesses at work.							
I prefer predictability to spontaneity.							

	A	B	C	D	E	F	G
Most criticism comes from jealousy.							
Reorganizations in my company make me nervous.							

	A	B	C	D	E	F	G
I feel compelled to succeed at everything.							
Businesses that succeed do so because they discover a "shortcut."							

	A	B	C	D	E	F	G
I avoid conflict with others at work.							
In most cases, if you act as if everything is fine, it will be.							

	A	B	C	D	E	F	G
It is better to stick with what you know will work than to try something you've never done before.							
In many business situations, it is better to hire an expert than to do the job yourself.							

	A	B	C	D	E	F	G
Sometimes I secretly feel that I was promoted to my current position because of some type of mistake.							
Most bosses will take advantage of you if you let them.							

	A	B	C	D	E	F	G
Success often depends on how I manage others' perception of myself.							
I rarely challenge my boss even when I feel that he or she is wrong.							

	A	B	C	D	E	F	G
Newer is not necessarily better and can be more trouble than it is worth.							
Powerful executives can ruin your career if their personal gain is at stake.							

	A	B	C	D	E	F	G
Winning is all that matters.							
I would have a hard time respecting a boss that was much younger than I.							

	A	B	C	D	E	F	G
I find it difficult to tell the truth when I know it will disappoint someone.							
I try to cut older coworkers some slack.							

	A	B	C	D	E	F	G
Luck plays a big part in success.							
Never contradict a person in power, or you will suffer for it.							

	A	B	C	D	E	F	G
Consistency is the secret to success.							
The longer a person is out of college, the more obsolete he or she becomes.							

	A	B	C	D	E	F	G
My business title is important to me.							
I worry about not getting my fair share.							

	A	B	C	D	E	F	G
Climbing the corporate ladder has a lot to do with being in the right place at the right time.				□			
I could really go places if I were ten years younger.						□	

| It is important for me to "keep up appearances" even when I don't feel like it. | | □ | | | | | |
| I keep an eye out for anyone trying to rip me off. | | | | | | | □ |

| Order is always preferable to chaos. | | | □ | | | | |
| Financial ruin is equivalent to a ruined life. | | | | | | | □ |

| I get nervous when presenting to higher-level executives. | | | | | □ | | |
| Older workers just don't have as much stamina as younger workers. | | | | | | □ | |

| It is best not to dwell on bad news. | | | | □ | | | |
| In the final analysis, earning a decent living is more important than liking what I do. | | | | | | | □ |

	A	B	C	D	E	F	G
I act differently when my boss is around.							
Financial security is the primary reason why I work.							

	A	B	C	D	E	F	G
New college hires are just more comfortable with these new technologies.							
The sad truth about success is that for every person who wins, someone else usually loses.							

	A	B	C	D	E	F	G
Column Totals							

Scoring

When you have finished with all pairs of statements, total the number of check marks in each column and write that total in the line labeled "Column Totals." Remember to include all twenty-one pairs in your total.

Your answers to this questionnaire tell you which of your fears have the greatest potential to affect your career. Each of the column totals represents your score on a fear. The scores on each type of fear are determined by entering your column totals in the corresponding rows in the Fear Susceptibility Inventory Score Sheet. The higher the score, the more that fear is likely to have an effect on your executive career.

Because this questionnaire forces you to choose between two equally fearful statements, the results do not indicate that you necessarily entertain the fears with the highest scores. The result shows which of these seven fears has the greatest *potential* to affect your career.

After scoring your questionnaire, pay particular attention to the chapters in this section of the book that correspond with your highest scores.

FEAR SUSCEPTIBILITY INVENTORY SCORE SHEET

Column	Fear	Total
A	Fear of Inadequacy	
B	Fear of Rejection	
C	Fear of the Unknown	
D	Fear of Reality	
E	Fear of Authority	
F	Fear of Aging	
G	Fear of Scarcity	

THREE

Fear of Inadequacy: What If I Fail?

The fear of inadequacy is one of the two strongest fears affecting modern executives. The more demanding the business world becomes, the greater the temptation to fear one's perceived inadequacy to meet the challenges.

The fear of inadequacy is certainly not new to those who wish to achieve great things. In fact, most of the ancient stories about conquering heroes are full of warnings about the pitfalls of fearing inadequacy. Let's consider one of these stories: the story of Samson, the hero who wished himself to be infallible.

Samson: The Hero

Samson was born to an Israelite woman who had long been barren. In gratitude for being given a son, she sanctified the child as a Nazarite—one who would not cut his hair, eat unclean meat, or drink wine. Samson, it was believed, would help deliver the Israelites from their forty years of slavery to the Philistines.

Samson grew into a very strong and determined young man. Much to his parents' displeasure, he refused the custom of marrying an Israelite and instead chose to marry the daughter of a Philistine.

Nothing stood in his way and the stories of his strength were numerous. In one particular instance, Samson killed a lion with his bare hands. Later, he returned to the lion and found bees and honey in the carcass. He then stole the honey from the bees and took it home to his parents. Samson knew no fear.

The precocious Samson posed a riddle to the men of his town, taunting them by saying: "Out of the eater came forth meat, and out of the strong came forth sweetness." But none of the men were able to answer the riddle.

Fearing Samson's wrath if they didn't answer the riddle, the men approached Samson's wife and said "Entice thy husband that he may declare unto us the riddle, lest we burn thee and thy father's house with fire." Samson's wife, frightened by the threats, eventually told the secret of the riddle to the town's men. Samson, angered by their tactics, went to town and slew thirty men. But when he returned, he discovered his wife had left him for a friend.

Samson tried to win back his wife with gifts of the harvest, but it was to no avail. Her father defended her against Samson saying, "I verily thought that thou hadst utterly hated her; therefore I gave her to thy companion." Enraged that the Philistine family had treated him this way, he set fire to standing corn of the Philistines and burnt up all their corn, olives, and vineyards.

The Israelite men, fearing retribution from the Philistines, bound Samson with the intention of delivering him to the Philistine army that was now assembling. But Samson broke free and with the "jawbone of an ass" he slaughtered a thousand of the Philistines. After that episode, the Philistines left Samson alone for twenty years.

In time, Samson fell in love with the beautiful Delilah. The Philistines, still secretly plotting retribution, prodded Delilah to discover the source of Samson's great strength. Samson, loath to divulge the secret, told Delilah that he would be helpless if he were bound with "several green widths that were never dried." Then, the lords of the Philistines came and bound him, but he broke free.

Again, Delilah asked him of his strength and twice more he lied to her. And she continued to press him for the answer until "his soul was vexed unto death." Finally he said, "There hath not come a razor upon my head; for I have been a Nazarite from my mother's womb: if I be shaven, then my strength will go from me, and I shall become weak, and be like any other man."

Delilah then went to the lords of the Philistines, who paid her money for the secret to Samson's strength. Then she returned to Samson and, when he was asleep, shaved his head. Indeed, Samson was now powerless and the Philistines blinded him, bound him in fetters of brass, and threw him into prison.

After some time, Samson's hair began to grow back and with it returned his strength. Unaware of Samson's renewed powers, his captors were indulging in a feast at the temple of the god of Dagon. As was their custom they called for a prisoner to come "make sport" before them. So it was that Samson was brought into the temple, filled with feasting Philistines. Samson said to his captors, "Suffer me that I may feel the pillars whereupon the house standeth, that I may lean upon them." And they did as he requested.

His strength fully returned, and Samson pulled the pillars of the temple down, killing himself and the three thousand people in the temple.

The tragic plight of Samson is the plight of all who act upon the advice of the infallible hero. By covering your weaknesses with mighty displays of strength, you create an illusion that becomes the target of your enemies. The more energy you give to your heroic image, the louder your invitation for confrontation and ultimate defeat becomes. You may finally prevail, but as was true for Samson, the last victory may cost you everything.

Like the Samson myth in Judeo-Christian culture, the story of the boisterous strength and tragic ending of the infallible hero appears in many cultures. In the Norse traditions it is the story of Siegfried; in the Greek mythology it is Theseus and Sisyphus; and in Native American culture it is Hiawatha. In each of these stories the Hero's stalwart appearance hides his one inevitable weakness. Rather than acknowledge and manage this weakness, the Hero always appears hell-bent on covering it up. In the end, it is the Hero's overblown image that entices his enemies to find this one, critical weakness.

THE INFALLIBLE EXECUTIVE

The infallible hero who is driven by a fear of inadequacy is alive and well in today's business world. The fast-moving, highly competitive modern corporation puts immense pressure on executives to be infallible superheroes. The expectations for the executive's performance are high and relentless, and if you can't meet those expectations, there are many others waiting in the wings who are willing to try.

So we try to be all things to all people. We try to be perfect. We try to excel at everything. We convince ourselves that in order to become a "leader" we must be the June Cleaver of executives—always prepared, always doing the right thing, and always making it look effortless. Or worse, we become aggressive bullies, hitting others over the head with our strengths and constantly "blowing our own trumpet."

At the core of our fantasy about being an infallible hero is the fear of inadequacy. We fear ourselves to be weak, and therefore spend our time trying to prove to ourselves and others that we are strong. Our fantasy of perfection is driven by a belief in our own inadequacy.

When we allow ourselves to become the infallible hero-executive we convince ourselves that we must be the best, the absolute best at *everything*. We must always be in control. We can never admit failure, never be seen as vulnerable, and must always be the winner.

What drives you isn't genuine concern for the success of the company, but an overwhelming need to prove to yourself that you are capable, worthwhile, and deserving of success. Privately, you suffer from the treacherous belief that you are insufficient, untalented, and inadequate, so you try to prove to yourself and others that this isn't so. Every interaction, every project is seen as a battle—an opportunity to prove, once again, that you are capable and worthwhile.

> As your self-confidence grows, fear of failing or the desire to always play it safe will diminish.[1]
> Terry Murray, CEO, Fleet Financial Group, Inc.

To cover up your feared inadequacies, you create a facade of super capability. Not only must you be the winner, you must talk about your great victories and prowess. It is very important to you that others believe the heroic image you have created. However, underneath it all, you are terrified that others will discover you to be a fake. You fear that they will uncover your charade and see that you are, at heart, what you believe yourself to be: inadequate.

All of this leads to something very troubling: You abuse your strengths and ignore your weaknesses. Since you are focused on being infallible, you fail to take a true inventory of your talents. Your weaknesses threaten you, so you ignore them and hope they will disappear.

This was precisely the downfall of Samson, as it is with all who are under the sway of the fear of inadequacy. Samson irresponsibly abused his strength, and in the process wreaked havoc among the Philistines, engendering their anger. Was it necessary to kill those thirty men? Or to set fire to fields of corn and orchards of olive trees?

Samson failed to acknowledge that the strength of his person lay in his *physical* strength only. In fact, he was not infallible. Nevertheless, he persistently overused his strength in an attempt to prove that he had no weaknesses.

But Samson did have weaknesses, including a distinct lack of finesse when it came to working with other people, and no amount of strutting and flexing could change this. Samson fell to the wiles of Delilah because he failed to protect himself against his other weakness—the fact that his strength was entirely dependent on his hair. He took no precautionary measures to protect those magical locks, even after Delilah discovered his secret. Instead, he was so determined to prove himself infallible, he failed to deal rationally with his weaknesses.

MONTGOMERY WARD

The list of executives who have succumbed to the fear of inadequacy is regrettably long. Near the top of that list is certainly Sewell Lee Avery.

In 1960, *Time* magazine printed the obituary of Sewell Lee Avery, the former head of Montgomery Ward, by starting with Avery's own words: "If anybody ventures to differ with me, I throw them out the window."

Avery, a successful top executive from the time he was twenty-one, once enjoyed the title of "the greatest business-man of the generation." During the economic turmoil of the Great Depression, Avery did what many thought impossible: He built a giant empire out of thirty small-time gypsum firms. Out of a motley array, he formed a $60 million plaster com-pany called U.S. Gypsum, which by 1936 dominated the indus-try. To accomplish such a miracle, Avery had slashed the costs of each firm he purchased and hoarded every extra penny of revenue—a strategy that helped U.S. Gypsum grow during a period when most companies were badly strapped for cash.

Convinced of his infallibility, Avery left U.S. Gypsum in 1939 and took total control of Montgomery Ward, assuming both the presidency and the chairmanship of the board. In-volving himself in virtually every aspect and at every level of the organization, Avery went to work, implementing his ideas. Unwilling to listen to any advice that contradicted his plan, he followed a ruthless, penny-pinching policy, paring Ward's budgets to the bone and eliminating dividends to sharehold-ers. Throughout the twenties, Ward had been primarily a mail-order catalog business aimed at farmers and rural customers, but Avery decided to change that in favor of more retail stores. He trimmed the mail-order divisions and added higher-priced product lines. In his usual brusque style he proclaimed: "We no longer depend on hicks and yokels. We now sell a lot more than overalls and manure-proof shoes."

Unfortunately, Avery's fanatical frugality and monarchi-cal plans began the demise of Montgomery Ward. While Avery was hoarding cash, Sears and other competing chains were expanding rapidly. By 1950, Ward had experienced dra-matic decreases in revenues and profits.

Perhaps his biggest error was his complete reluctance to negotiate a labor contract with the Congress of Industrial Or-ganizations (CIO). In spite of heavy pressure from the War Labor Board of 1944, he refused to make peace with his work-force, convinced that he could force the union out of Mont-gomery Ward.

Avery refused to listen to advice about compromise, in-cluding direct orders from President Franklin D. Roosevelt to settle or relinquish control of the company. Still convinced of his invincibility, he persisted until, under the supervision of

Attorney General Francis Biddle, he was physically picked up in his chair and placed on the street.

Avery's difficulties first began when he convinced himself and the board of directors at Montgomery Ward that his success at U.S. Gypsum would transfer to a national retail business. Despite the fact that retail is an entirely different industry, he rode in like a white knight to save the day. Why listen to the retail analysts who were continually criticizing his strategy? He was on a mission to prove to himself and the world that he was "the greatest businessman of the generation." While Avery had many strengths as an executive, he erred in thinking that he could do *anything* he set his mind to do. Further, he failed to see that his major weaknesses revolved around managing people, labor contracts, and corporate expansion. He was talented at helping a company pare down, but knew little about managing growth.[2]

Had Avery not been under the sway of the fear of inadequacy, he would have confidently used his strengths and then carefully surrounded himself with competent staff who could have handled his weaknesses. Such a strategy would have allowed him to shine and Montgomery Ward to prosper. Instead, he used the company as a proving ground for his fantasy of infallibility, and in the process destroyed his own career and severely damaged the company.

WORKAHOLICS

Infallible executives usually work extremely long hours. They are classic workaholics, sacrificing all other aspects of their personal lives to spend all their time and energy at work. Time off is usually spent strategizing and thinking about work. It is not uncommon for them to schedule meetings in the early morning or evening hours, expecting that others keep the same pace. They plan vacations around work activities, if they take them at all. Only in cases of exceptional illness will infallible executives take time off—and even then they work from home.

WINNING IS ALL THAT MATTERS

More concerned for his career than the long-term interest of the company, the infallible executive exacts a heavy toll.

While he gets things done, he stops at nothing to get the job accomplished. So committed is he to his success and reputation, he spends whatever time, money, and talent it takes to make the job appear a success once he has begun. He is not one to admit failure, even when that failure was due to unexpected circumstances. He can be excessively controlling and often uses up very creative and talented staff members in a short time. The infallible executive is inflexible and intolerant of differing viewpoints, and views his staff as an extension of his arm in carrying out his agenda. He is slow to change his opinions and actively thwarts any move that might reduce his power. In short, he is a one-person company who is in business to promote himself. Whatever resources and power the company gives him are used to his advantage.

The executive driven by a fear of inadequacy is blinded to the humanity of others, choosing to view them as objects, or modules, to be moved about the game board of the organization—a game he is determined to win at all costs. No one, including infallible executives, can get ahead without enlisting the help of others, so these executives may turn on considerable charm, sympathy, or understanding if necessary to win over someone as a useful ally. When that pawn has served his purposes and is of no further use, he may be coolly discarded.

The infallible executive often assumes that everyone else is out to prove himself infallible, too, and he has little or no respect for those who are more willing to achieve compromise. He often sees others as wanting something from him and is highly sensitive to being used by someone else. Interactions with others in the company usually take the form of a trade-off: "If I give you what you need, what do I get in return?" Conversely, when he needs something from others, he assumes that others will require some trade-off from him. It is not unusual for the infallible executive to stockpile power and resources to use as bargaining chips when needed.

PUTTING A SPIN ON SETBACKS

Warren, a manufacturing manager, headed the largest manufacturing division of a major defense contractor. Not only did he have the largest staff, he controlled most of the company's premier product lines, including several highly touted new products. His boss was nearing retirement, and Warren had his eye on the boss' job, the highest-ranking manufacturing job in the company. To raise his potential for the job in a company that was heavily dependent on federal regulations, Warren arranged a highly visible, one-year, corporate-sponsored fellowship in the Department of Defense. Several months after arriving in Washington, something went very wrong (no one seems to know exactly what happened), and Warren found himself needing his old job back nearly six months earlier than planned.

Upon his return to the company, however, Warren was given the only manufacturing job open, which was in one of the oldest divisions in the company, a much smaller and far less prestigious position. To try to correct the perception of this move as a setback, Warren created and spread the story that he had been called back from Washington early to solve the division's manufacturing problems (of which no one was aware) and to broaden his experience before accepting the vice presidential position.

The infallible executive can put a spin on almost any event if it is to his advantage. Like Warren, he can take any outcome and spin a story that fulfills the plot he has invented. Should events turn out less than desirable, he becomes the master of damage control, issuing virtual press releases by the hour until the danger is passed. The story is easily recognizable; it has an airtight goodness about it that makes it seem very real. The infallible executive must always appear to be in control and successful, even heroic.

EMPIRE BUILDING

Using his well-practiced power techniques, the infallible executive will "build an empire" if given the opportunity. There are several compelling reasons why he must acquire more people, money, and power. By finding more power and importance in the organization, he makes himself indispensable to the company and ensures that his projects are funded, adequately staffed, and ultimately successful. Furthermore, more power gives him the opportunity to hire and develop people who will agree with his point of view and carry out his ideas.

Judy left her job at an upstart high-tech company to take a better paying job with a public agency that had a long reputation for being a quintessential bureaucracy. Once Judy got her bearings in the organization, she discovered that a fellow director, one who also reported to her boss, had a rather strangely structured department. It was a hodgepodge of functions and jobs that the director had slowly and carefully accumulated over the years. There was no logic to the boundaries between Judy's department and her colleague's.

Judy suggested to her colleague that a reorganization might be more logical, not to mention more efficient. The suggestion ignited a storm of controversy, not the least of which was the passive withholding of all information to Judy's department. Time and time again her colleague silently sabotaged her. Eventually the colleague was successful at having Judy relocated to a site that was miles away from the corporate headquarters. Judy had most definitely underestimated the importance of boundaries and the vigor with which the infallible executive protects his image.

Gaining high visibility within the company is critical to the infallible executive's fulfillment of his infallible image. He pushes himself to achieve not merely for achievement's sake, but for the recognition and praise that accompanies that achievement. Without visibility, there can be no recognition.

BREAKING THE CYCLE OF FEAR

Step 1: Acknowledge and confront the irrational beliefs that underlie your fear of inadequacy.

Irrational Belief #1: I can't have weaknesses.

Regardless of how wonderful your strengths may be, you still have weaknesses. *Every successful executive has weaknesses.* There are some tasks at which you will never excel. No amount of overexertion, money, or positive thinking will change this.

You must go further: You must *embrace* these weaknesses. The question is not *whether* you are weak, but *how* are you weak? By embracing your weaknesses without shame, you can then protect yourself from them. What do you usually do poorly? Allow yourself to bring those weaknesses into your conscious awareness. Without condemning yourself or trying to "fix" them, learn to accept those weaknesses. Try to see the dignity of your weakness.

As you touch your weaknesses, you do not deny them or "sweep them under the rug." Instead, you see them for what they are. Ask yourself: "Can I hire someone else who has strengths in the areas of my weakness? Can I eliminate that aspect of my job that plays to my weaknesses? Is there some minimal effort I need to expend to protect myself from those weaknesses?"

> You will make mistakes which, in the end, will have helped you grow. Don't be afraid of letting that happen. You have to take chances and make decisions. The right ones will put you ahead and give you confidence. Those that are wrong will at least teach you and allow you to make smaller steps toward your success.[3]
>
> Arthur Crandall, President, Standard Copy

I remember once working with a product development executive who was considered to be a genius in the field of textiles. She had a phenomenal eye for fabric and spent much of her time combing the markets in the Pacific Rim, looking for new fabrics that could be made into products for the market back in the United States. Her list of product successes was long and consistent.

Her primary weakness, however, was in working with the product managers back home. She was the classic bull in a china shop and, as best as I could tell, had been for most of her life. Despite her successful product decisions, her gruff nature threatened to ruin her career. No one wanted to work with her, and several key executives were eager to see her leave the company.

In our work together, we never attempted to make this executive into a "people person." In fact, we didn't even work on her relationship skills. Instead, we worked on helping her learn to be silent. We could not change her brusque personality, but we could minimize the damage it might create.

Every time she felt the urge to correct, belittle, or verbally attack another executive, she was encouraged to practice the art of being silent. Over many months of work, she became quite good at controlling her outbursts by simply keeping quiet. She didn't learn to be empathic or congenial; she learned to sit back in her chair and remain quiet until the aggressive urge passed.

Managing her weakness not only saved her job, but probably saved her career. She will never be the model of interpersonal relationships—that isn't her strength. Instead, she learned to keep her weaknesses from defeating her while she capitalized on her considerable talent as a product development executive.

When you deny your weaknesses, you only give them the power to harm yourself. Unattended they can grow larger and ultimately defeat you. When you embrace those weaknesses, you immediately defuse them of power and prevent them from interfering with all the good things your talents bring to you.

Irrational Belief #2: Mistakes are valueless.

It's true that no one likes to make mistakes, but it is even truer that we all make them. Mistakes often carry greater informational value than do successes. Mistakes force you to investigate what went wrong and to try again if you want to be successful at a task. Immediate success, on the other hand, only tells you that you did something right.

> Lou Brock holds two baseball records: the most stolen bases and the most times being thrown out trying to steal bases. Lee Iacocca was fired by Ford Motor Company, then he went to work and saved Chrysler. I'm not advising you to go out and fail, but when you fail at something—and you probably will—learn from it.[4]
>
> William G. Mays, President,
> Mays Chemical Company, Inc.

Michael Barach was the vice president of a $100 million furniture company when he left his job to become the head of a start-up company called Cartoon Corner—a competitor to the Disney Store. Three years after he took the position, the company dissolved and Barach was faced with what appeared to be a glaring failure on his résumé. He was now the former chief executive of a bankrupt company.

But the venture capital firm of Bessemer Venture Partners saw things differently. It saw an executive who had learned some hard lessons in managing a business and hired Barach to head up its Internet start-up Mothernature.com. Today, he is making a success of his company based on the difficult lessons he learned at Cartoon Corner.

Barach says of his experience, "I am much more humble and paranoid." The lessons he learned from his own career setback have encouraged him to hire other senior executives who have had similar experiences. "All my senior managers had something happen along the way," he says.[5]

Irrational Belief #3: My worth is a function of my achievements.

Most successful executives come face-to-face with this irrational belief. After all, if your job is to continuously achieve results, it becomes an easy leap to start judging your own worth (and the worth of others) based on how successful you are. I'm not about to tell you that achievements aren't important, because they are. What I am saying is that your worth as a human being has nothing to do with your success. Regardless of what you achieve, who you are does not change. You are not a better human being because you have risen to the top of the organization, and likewise, you are not a lesser person because you never made it out of the mailroom.

Why is this so important? Because one day you will fail—and fail miserably. When that day comes, you will never find the confidence to pull yourself up and learn from your mistakes as long as you hold to the irrational belief that your accomplishments define who you are. It feels great to pat yourself on the back and believe that you are somehow superior when you succeed, but if you do this you must also condemn yourself harshly when you fail. You must learn to accept that success is wonderful and important, but it has no bearing on the essence of you.

When you confront this irrational belief, it takes the punch out of fearing inadequacy. You see, the real pain within the fear of inadequacy is in believing that you are a lesser human being if you fail. Therefore, you *cannot* fail, and you come to fear failure. When you realize that success isn't all there is to life, and that there is a wonderful life even after the worst of failures, you let yourself off the hook. When you do, you actually free yourself to enjoy the journey to success.

Enjoying the journey is no small part of discovering the real joy of life. As we will see later in this chapter, there are no destinations in life. There is no single place at which you can arrive that will make you completely happy and fulfilled. Those things come from the *journey*, not from achieving a goal.

Step 2: Make a conscious effort to push past the fear of inadequacy even though you continue to feel it.

One of the exercises I often use with executives is this: For one entire week, stop selling yourself. Make a list of all the ways you are constantly proving to others how great you are at your job, how correct your opinions are, and how you have not made any mistakes. Think about it very carefully and write down your list. Now, make a conscious effort for the next week not to do any of those things.

If you do this, you will immediately notice that your fear of inadequacy begins to increase. As you are driving your car or lying awake in the middle of the night, you may worry about how things are falling apart. But stick to the plan until the week is over.

What you'll realize by the end of the week is that much of that worrying was completely unnecessary. You don't have to be perfect, and since you aren't anyway, you'll find that the world doesn't fall apart. In fact, I'm betting that your job becomes easier as you stop spending so much time trying to prove your own infallibility. It's like dropping a great weight that has slowed you down. If you continue to push past your feeling of fear, you'll find that not only are you accomplishing more, your fear has disappeared.

Step 3: Take positive action in the direction of your fear.

The most positive action you can make is to identify the smallest unit of the task you can manage. For example, if you've been told to prepare a thorough evaluation of all two thousand stores that your company owns, break the task down into the smallest unit that you feel comfortable in accomplishing. Now, do only that unit. Perhaps it is the evaluation of a single store. Perhaps the evaluation of a small district of stores.

There is great wisdom in only doing the smallest unit. It's like the founders of Alcoholics Anonymous wrote many years ago: "just for today." For many, the smallest unit of sobriety that they can think of handling is one day. If they even allow themselves to consider the mammoth task of a lifetime of sobriety, they would be defeated before they started. The wonderful thing about "just for today" is that for millions those days have added up to an entire lifetime of sobriety.

So what's the big challenge that is haunting you? Stop focusing on the whole of it and focus on one small part that you can do. When you are finished with that, focus only on another part. In no time, you will have made more progress than you imagined possible toward your larger goal.

NOTES

1. Michael Ames, *Pathways to Success* (San Francisco: Berrett Koehler Books, 1994).
2. Manfred DeVries, *Unstable at the Top* (New York: Mentor, 1987).
3. Ames, *Pathways to Success*, 36.
4. Ibid, 90.
5. Leslie Kaufman, "Failed at Your Last Job? Wonderful! You're Hired." *New York Times*, 6 October 1999.

FOUR

Fear of Rejection: What If I Don't Make It to the Inner Circle?

The fear of rejection is the second strongest fear that influences the modern executive, and it is often intertwined with the fear of inadequacy. If you have a desire to make it to the top, you first need to be accepted by those at the top. And what if you aren't? That question is enough to strike fear in the hearts of many aspiring executives.

The fear of rejection isn't limited to executives. It's everywhere in life—and in history. Take a look at one of the most enlightening stories ever written about the fear of rejection.

THE EMPEROR'S NEW CLOTHES

Many years ago there lived an Emperor, who was so excessively fond of grand new clothes that he spent all his money upon them, that he might be very fine. He did not care about his soldiers, nor about the theater, and only liked to drive out and show his new clothes. He had a coat for every hour of the day; and just as they say of a king, "He is in council," so they always said of him, "The Emperor is in the wardrobe."

In the great city in which he lived it was always very merry; every day came many strangers; one day two rogues came: They gave themselves out as weavers, and declared they could weave the finest stuff any one could imagine. Not only were their colors and patterns, they said, uncommonly beautiful, but the clothes made of the stuff possessed the wonderful quality that they became invisible to any one who was unfit for the office he held, or was incorrigibly stupid.

"Those would be capital clothes!" thought the Emperor. "If I wore those, I should be able to find out what men in my empire are not fit for the places they have; I could tell the clever from the dunces. Yes, the stuff must be woven for me directly!"

And he gave the two rogues a great deal of cash in hand, that they might begin their work at once.

As for them, they put up two looms, and pretended to be working; but they had nothing at all on their looms. They at once demanded the finest silk and the costliest gold; this they put into their own pockets, and worked at the empty looms till late into the night.

"I should like to know how far they have got on with the stuff," thought the Emperor. But he felt quite uncomfortable when he thought that those who were not fit for their offices could not see it. He believed, indeed, that he had nothing to fear for himself, but yet he preferred first to send someone else to see how matters stood. All the people in the city knew what peculiar power the stuff possessed, and all were anxious to see how bad or how stupid their neighbors were.

"I will send my honest old Minister to the weavers," thought the Emperor. "He can judge best how the stuff looks, for he has sense, and no one understands his office better than he."

Now the good old Minister went out into the hall where the two rogues sat working at the empty looms.

"Mercy on us!" thought the old Minister, and he opened his eyes wide. "I cannot see anything at all!" But he did not say this.

Both the rogues begged him to be so good as to

come nearer, and asked if he did not approve of the colors and the pattern. Then they pointed to the empty loom, and the poor old Minister went on opening his eyes; but he could see nothing, for there was nothing to see.

"Mercy!" thought he, "can I indeed be so stupid? I never thought that, and not a soul must know it. Am I not fit for my office? No, it will never do for me to tell that I could not see the stuff."

"Don't you say anything to it?" asked one, as he went on weaving.

"O, it is charming—quite enchanting!" answered the old Minister, as he peered through his spectacles. "What a fine pattern, and what colors! Yes, I shall tell the Emperor that I am very much pleased with it."

"Well, we are glad of that," said both the weavers; and then they named the colors, and explained the strange pattern. The old Minister listened attentively, that he might be able to repeat it when the Emperor came. And he did so.

The Emperor soon sent again, dispatching another honest officer of the court, to see how the weaving was going on, and if the stuff would soon be ready. He fared just like the first: he looked and looked, but, as there was nothing to be seen but the empty looms, he could see nothing.

"Is not that a pretty piece of stuff?" asked the two rogues; and they displayed and explained the handsome pattern which was not there at all.

"I am not stupid!" thought the man: "must be my good office, for which I am not fit. It is funny enough, but I must not let it be noticed." And so he praised the stuff which he did not see, and expressed his pleasure at the beautiful colors and charming pattern. "Yes, it is enchanting," he told the Emperor.

All the people in the town were talking of the gorgeous stuff. The Emperor wished to see it himself while it was still upon the loom.

"What's this?" thought the Emperor. "I can see nothing at all! That is terrible. Am I stupid? Am I not fit to be the Emperor? That would be the most dreadful thing that could happen to me."

"O, it is *very* pretty!" he said aloud. "It has our highest approbation." And he nodded in a contented way, and gazed at the empty loom, for he would not say that he saw nothing. The whole suite whom he had with him looked and looked, and saw nothing, any more than the rest; but, like the Emperor, they said, "That *is* pretty!" and counseled him to wear the splendid new clothes for the first time at the great procession that was presently to take place. "It is splendid, excellent!" went from mouth to mouth. On all sides there seemed to be general rejoicing, and the Emperor gave the rogues the title of Imperial Court Weavers.

The whole night before the morning on which the procession was to take place, the rogues were up, and kept more than sixteen candles burning. They pretended to take the stuff down from the loom; they made cuts in the air with great scissors; they sewed with needles without thread; and at last they said, "Now the clothes are ready!"

"Will your Imperial Majesty please to condescend to take off your clothes?" said the rogues; "then we will put on you the new clothes here in front of the great mirror."

The Emperor took off his clothes, and the rogues pretended to put on him each new garment as it was ready; and the Emperor turned round and round before the mirror.

"O, how well they look! How capitally they fit!" said all. "What a pattern! What colors! That *is* splendid dress!"

"Well, I am ready," replied the Emperor. "Does it not suit me well?" And then he turned again to the mirror, for he wanted it to appear as if he contemplated his adornment with great interest.

The two chamberlains, who were to carry the train, stooped down with their hands toward the floor, just as if they were picking up the mantle; then they pretended to be holding something in the air.

They did not dare let it be noticed that they saw nothing.

So the Emperor went in procession under the rich canopy, and every one in the streets said, "How incomparable are the Emperor's new clothes! What a train he has to his mantle! How it fits him!" No one would let it be perceived that he could see nothing, for that would have shown that he was not fit for his office, or was very stupid. No clothes of the Emperor's had ever had such a success as these.

"But he has nothing on!" a little child cried out at last.

"Just hear what the innocent says!" said the father: and one whispered to another what the child had said.

"But he has nothing on!" said the whole people at length. That touched the Emperor, for it seemed to him that they were right; but he thought within himself, "I must go through with the procession." And so he held himself a little higher, and the chamberlains held on tighter than ever, and carried the train that did not exist at all.[1]

STANDING NAKED

Every one of us has at some point stood and stared at the naked emperor, and then declared the beauty of his imaginary robes. We are at our core social creatures; we want to fit in, to be a part of the in crowd, to be accepted by our peers. At times, that need so overwhelms us that we abandon reality, just as all the villagers and ministers did when they admired the emperor's nonexistent clothes.

The desire to be accepted and loved by others is universal. It is a good and healthy need that causes us to treat others with fairness and compassion. Without a doubt, it is the social "grease" that makes an organization run smoothly.

The drive to be accepted is particularly strong for the aspiring executive. The executive *must* fit in and be likable, at least to his or her superiors and peers. Not being accepted by one's peers is as quick a way to be fired as any. In fact, experience is that the majority of all executive firings are the result of executives not fitting in with the larger team.

But where there is a strong drive, there can also be an equally strong fear. *What if I don't fit in? What if they don't like me? What if I can't be a part of the team?* These questions can loom large and come to overwhelm the aspiring executive's actions. Subtly there is a shift from *What is the right business decision?* to *What will make them like me more?*

When your need for acceptance so consumes you that the thought of rejection strikes this fear within, you have crossed the line into danger. This fear can be strong and powerful, particularly in the modern competitive corporation, where it can lead entire organizations to deny reality and, instead, support a delusion. No one dares to criticize the actions of another. No one will go against the social current. Everyone tries to be an approving team member. Even when the Emperor has no clothes, no one dares to snicker.

Consider what happened when this was the case for our country's chief executive.

PRESIDENT JOHNSON AND VIETNAM

Perhaps in no other presidential administration was there a stronger example of the fear of rejection than in that of President Lyndon B. Johnson. Johnson has been characterized by numerous journalists and biographers as "an extraordinarily aggressive and insensitive leader, who made such excessive and humiliating demands on everyone who came in frequent contact with him that he was cordially disliked, if not hated."[2] He demanded that his close advisers and cabinet members support his personal agenda, and he had little tolerance for dissenting opinions. In the Johnson administration, success was defined by conforming to the norms set by the president.

The consequences of not conforming were real and clear: the loss of your job. By the end of Johnson's tenure in office, all but one of his advisers had been individually replaced. He had created a working environment that preyed upon his advisers' fear of rejection. Only those who were willing to play the role of the yes-man could survive.

The detrimental effects of the yes-man syndrome affected the entire country during the gradual escalation of the Vietnam War. Despite a continual stream of evidence from virtually every branch of the government that escalation of the war would not succeed, Johnson and his advisers ignored what they were told. Instead, they pursued a course of action that they hoped would fulfill Johnson's primary goal: not to be the first President to lose a war. Since there was little support in the country for the war, Johnson couldn't muster the military force to crush the Communists in the north, making instead a series of decisions that had the effect of prolonging the war so that he and his political party would not be blamed for allowing a red flag to rise over Saigon. As the *New York Times* political analyst Daniel Ellsberg wrote, "measures were taken not as last steps but rather as holding actions, adequate to avoid defeat in the short run but long shots so far as ultimate success was concerned" designed to avoid the "political and personal consequences of charges of 'softness on Communism.'"[3]

What is most interesting is that Johnson's advisers all had access to credible information that indicated a course of action just the opposite of how they were proceeding. Ellsberg writes that Johnson's advisers neglected to call his attention to the dangers of bypassing Congress, of allowing official military statements that describe the enemy forces as defeated to be issued during a lull in the fighting when those forces were readying for a major offensive, and of accepting recommendations from the Pentagon to "draft and spend and kill and suffer casualties at the rate military will propose."[4]

Reports from the CIA, the State Department, and the Defense Department all showed a "persistent skepticism about proposals for improving [the long-run prospects of anti-Communist forces], a pessimism almost unrelieved, often stark—yet in retrospect, credibly realistic, frank, cogent."[5] Even on those occasions when major decisions were made to escalate the war, the President's advisers ignored reports that ran contrary to their mind-set. For example, in the fall of 1964, Operation Rolling Thunder (bombing of the North Vietnamese oil storage facilities) was initiated despite the fact that the entire intelligence community, according to the Department of Defense study, predicted that the bombing would not cripple Communist military operations. After a year and a half of continual bombing with no significant impact, the decision was made to step up the bombing, despite the CIA's repeated estimation that such an escalation would not "bring the enemy to the conference table."

Throughout the Johnson administration (1962–1968), the President and his advisers (affectionately called the "Tuesday Cabinet") formed a cohesive group that lacked critical debate. Bill Moyers, press secretary for the administration, says of his colleagues: "They tended to conduct the affairs of state almost as if they were a gentlemen's club, and the great decisions were often made in that warm camaraderie of a small board of directors deciding what the club's dues are going to be for the members next year."[6]

What has in retrospect emerged from the decision making of the Johnson administration is the picture of a strong fear of rejection. Johnson, afraid of losing the war and having his political career destroyed, did not tolerate any suggestion that victory in Vietnam was impossible given the political climate against the war in the United States. He surrounded himself with advisers who, afraid of being rejected from the tightly knit group, failed to pass on information that didn't conform to his wishes. Henry Graff, a historian who had the opportunity to interview Johnson and his advisers numerous times from 1965 to 1968, writes: "The men of the Tuesday Cabinet were loyal to each other, with a devotion compounded by mutual respect and common adversity. They soon learned . . . to listen selectively and to talk harmoniously even when in disagreement."[7]

It was the fear of rejection that ultimately led the Johnson administration into political demise. By 1968, he was so disliked for having extended what was seen as an aimless war that his own party encouraged him not to run for a second term, a highly unusual event considering the incumbent's usual advantage in an election. Johnson defeated himself by trying to avoid the rejection of the electorate. He was overcome by the fear of rejection.

A similar fate befell most of his cabinet and close advisers. With the exception of Secretary of State Dean Rusk, every cabinet member was replaced at least once during his term. White House Assistant McGeorge Bundy, Secretary of Defense

Robert McNamara, Chairman of the Joint Chiefs of Staff General Earl Wheeler, and Director of the CIA Richard Helms all suffered greatly for having been associated with the Johnson White House and its decisions regarding Vietnam.

Such is the fate of the executive who succumbs to the fear of rejection. He is so consumed with pleasing others he blinds himself to the reality of business, and as a result, alienates himself from the very people whose acceptance he craves.

President Johnson, ever fearful of being rejected by the American electorate, did what he thought would win their acceptance and secure his political ambitions. In turn, he surrounded himself with advisers who were eager to win his approval.

The fear of rejection in an organization has this kind of cascading effect. The executives who are determined to win the approval of their superiors often hire employees who display a strong willingness to seek their approval. These executives surround themselves with employees who, because they too are hungry for approval, are unwilling to contradict the boss even when they suspect he is wrong.

The fear of rejection is strong and seductive. You want to be accepted. You want the approval of your superiors. The problem arises when you go beyond desiring approval and are consumed by the fear of rejection. You clamp down on your relationships and refuse to allow anything to transpire that might cause you to be rejected. Your need for approval becomes overwhelmingly strong, even stronger than your desire to do good business. You trade off your own person to become the executive you think others want you to be. You discard your own talents and passion in order to play a role that you mistakenly believe will win the approval of others.

When this happens you do far more damage to your career than the imagined rejection would have ever created. By gradually abandoning your talents, you leave behind the power of your greatest assets. Instead of fulfilling the path you were meant to follow, you choose another path that you think will win approval.

In truth, the only path that will completely satisfy you is the path of integrity with your *whole* self. The difficult truth is that the path sometimes leads executives into situations that don't win the approval of others. Sometimes it means doing the right thing, even when it is unpopular. Sometimes it means going it alone. But ultimately it is the path that will lead you to your greatest success, because the power of authenticity is one of the greatest career boosters anyone can have.

When you choose to go down the road of approval and acceptance instead of following the direction determined by your own talents and passion, you have reached a critical point of career derailment. You have become more willing to seek the approval of others than to stand true to yourself, and consequently, you miss the opportunity for success that has been placed before you. You may win others' approval, but you have lost the greater victory of employing your talents toward your own fulfillment. Instead of allowing your talents to guide you, you are guided by fear.

For many of us, the beginnings of the fear of rejection go back to early childhood. As children we were all incredibly vulnerable and entirely dependent upon the goodwill of our parents for food and shelter. In early childhood, rejection by the parent is devastating.

Childhood neglect, either physical or emotional, is one source of the fear of rejection. That fear then becomes a significant life force as the child matures into an adult. Figures of authority become feared beings who must be pleased and whose approval is overwhelmingly important.

The fear of rejection, however, does not always begin with a child's parent. For some, it first appears on the school playground as the child desperately seeks to fit in with the other children. Rejection at that tender age can be traumatic and may cause the child to resolve that she will never experience the pain of rejection again.

Later on, in young adulthood, it continues as membership in clubs and fraternal orders. Those who are selected for membership reward themselves with camaraderie and sneer upon the "independents" who were rejected (a projection of their own fear of being rejected). The fear of rejection continues to grow through acceptance into the right college, the best job offers, and acquiring a high-ranking management position. In each of these situations, from the playground to the boardroom, the message of fear is the same: "To not be accepted is disastrous. Do whatever it takes to fit in."

As adults, nothing evokes the fear of rejection more than an impending evaluation of our work. Whether it be formal performance reviews or informal feedback, the fear of rejection can leap into the forefront of our minds, and cloud our thinking. That was the case in the story of the emperor's new clothes, when the emperor said, "If I wore those, I should be able to find out what men in my empire are not fit for the places they have; I could tell the clever from the dunces." It was the emperor's evaluation of competence that sparked the fear in his ministers and eventually in the whole kingdom.

FEEDBACK BECOMES AN ATTACK

Those who have not conquered their fear of rejection find evaluations of their work terribly threatening. When the fear is strong, they will do anything to avoid a negative evaluation, even if it means abandoning their own commitment to excellence to conform to a standard they imagine will win them a positive evaluation.

The fear of rejection is in no small part why some organizations continue to spiral further and further away from reality. Executives in the organization become completely focused on what they think is expected of them, not on what will help the organization succeed. When those perceived expectations depart from what would make the organization successful, the organization slowly drifts further away from success.

Brave executives in such an organization, who refuse to succumb to the fear of rejection, risk their jobs in the short run in order to buck the misguided tide. Standing face-to-face with the emperor and calling him nude isn't easy in the least—especially when the entire kingdom disagrees!

But in the long run, this is the stuff of which great executives are made. Sure, they may lose a job or two because they are unwilling to kowtow to the party line, but in the end, their courage in facing painful realities wins them great respect. During the later years of Richard Nixon's first term in office (before the Watergate fiasco), he was widely honored for bringing the Vietnam War to a close. Although it was clear to the public that we had not won the war (a public perception greatly feared by the Johnson administration), Nixon was respected for having ended the conflict. One can only imagine how different American politics might be today if President Johnson had not succumbed to the fear of rejection and had chosen to end rather than escalate the war.

The fear of rejection is far more widespread and subtle than you may think. Much of what passes for "being a team player" and "fitting into the corporate culture" is really just the plain old fear of being seen as different. Andrew Grove, the widely respected chairman of Intel, writes about just such a case that he observed:

> One of our divisional marketing managers recently asked for a meeting with me. A man in his mid-30's, he reports to a division general manager, who reports to the group general manager, who in turn reports to me. I know that this fellow works hard at his job, and also that he pays attention to his progress up the ladder. As he said quite openly when asking for the meeting, the purpose of the session was to have a "career checkup": He wanted to know if he was doing all the right things for the company to continue his rise through the ranks.
>
> Our discussion went smoothly at first. He told me of some things he had done in the past year that he was particularly proud of and a bit about what he planned to do. Then he asked what I thought he should be working on. I countered with another question: What were his strengths? He quickly replied that he prided himself on his organizational skills, his understanding of his product area and the market, and his rapport with the corporate sales force—the people who, while not under his authority, use his marketing strategies to sell the division's products. Next I asked where he thought he was lacking. After considerable hesitation, he gave an answer that didn't mean a whole lot to me: "I am afraid I don't provide enough leadership. . . ."
>
> A few weeks after my meeting with the man, I happened to see him in action. He was giving a presentation—an important one—to a group of cor-

porate sales managers, explaining his division's marketing plans for the next six months: what to sell, to whom, how, and for how much. His aim was to ensure that his products would receive a healthy "share of mind" among the sales managers, who sell products from all of Intel's divisions.

This was no piece of cake. As I listened from the back row, one sales manager after another raised objections to the plans being presented. "How can we sell against the competition if we don't have the such-and-such feature?" one demanded. "Unless we have a complete family to offer, we are wasting our time," another said. And so it went, each comment just stimulating another even more critical one.

The young marketing manager acted as if he basically agreed with the comments, even when they were obviously exaggerated. It seemed to me that the sales managers were mainly trying to make their own lives easier. The perfect product is easy to sell; no salesman enjoys having to make up for a product's imperfections by dint of extra work. But the marketing exec was so bent on appeasing this group that he just went with the flow, agreeing with whatever they said. When his time was up, he left behind a very disgruntled group of sales managers. . . .

What the marketing manager needed to do was make this ordinary group of salesmen commit themselves to do their extraordinary best in selling his imperfect and incomplete product line. The more his products were underdogs to the competition, the more he needed to elicit such a commitment. But he didn't rise to the occasion. His earlier comment about his lack of leadership skills was, unfortunately, quite correct, perhaps even more true than he realized.[8]

What undermined this marketing manager (in front of his company's CEO, no less!) was his fear of being rejected by the salesmen. Obviously, they were unhappy with the product; if he had taken the stance that Grove suggests, he would have risked alienating himself with the sales force. Instead, he tried to appease them, which only resulted in their increased frustration with what he had to say.

DRUNK ON CONSENSUS

In some companies, the fear of rejection is actually fostered. Major decisions are made by consensus, where everyone (and I do mean *everyone*) is given a chance to have input on the decision. What drives this practice is more often a fear of someone opposing the decision rather than an honest attempt to glean information from all the employees.

Let me describe it another way. How many times have you been asked to give "feedback" to a decision that you know has already been made privately? You know it won't matter what you say, and that the decision is a foregone conclusion, regardless of your input. You were simply asked your opinion so that you would be less likely to criticize the outcome.

Involving others can be extremely helpful in making management decisions. However, it is also important to realize that most decisions made by a committee tend to be either mediocre (a melting pot of opposing opinions) or radical and risky (*groupthink*: since no one person takes responsibility for the decision, the group is more willing to make decisions that are outlandish). Neither of these options is desirable.

The key to overcoming this form of the fear of rejection is to identify the decisions that will truly benefit from group input. Then, once that input is gathered, seriously consider all points expressed. When a decision doesn't need the input of others (who may be less qualified than you to make the decision) it is important to make the decision yourself.

UNWILLING TO TELL DANGEROUS TRUTHS

Those who strongly fear rejection can have a big influence on an entire organization. They can force the truth to take a backseat when the dressed-up, turbocharged version makes them look better. The problem with this approach is that over time it can distort the truth beyond recognition and cause executives to promise virtually anything that they believe their superiors want to hear.

Taken to an extreme, organizations have made major decisions based on promises that exist only on overhead transparencies, which were made by someone who wanted to look good. The result is not only bad decisions but also an erosion of trust among members of an organization. Eventually, those who so willingly stretch the truth are found out, and their careers are stymied. What started as an effort to gain acceptance turns out to be a surefire path to rejection.

TALK IS CHEAP

Another rather distasteful side effect of the fear of rejection is what psychologists call passive aggression. Passive aggression happens when a person appears to agree with you but acts differently. It is particularly angering to work with someone who is passive aggressive because they won't tell you what they *really* think. Instead, they tell you what they think you want to hear; then, when in another situation, they may completely reverse themselves if they think it will gain them acceptance among that group. Passive-aggressive types will publicly agree with the boss, and then privately do as they please. At the core of passive aggression is a strong fear of rejection.

BREAKING THE CYCLE OF FEAR

Step 1: Acknowledge and confront the irrational beliefs that underlie your fear of rejection.

Irrational Belief #1: Others have no need of what I offer.

The basic belief underlying the fear of rejection is that others have no need of your talents, or worse, that you have no talents to offer.

This belief creates a one-sided affair: "I need you to approve of me, but you don't need me." In contrast, the way of the executive who has conquered the fear of rejection is two sided: "I need you for your talent and you need me for mine." This is *interdependence,* and it is the nature of all productive relationships. With interdependence, both parties are equal participants. A relationship, whether with a person or a group, that is anything less than interdependent isn't worth having. The executive who trusts this interdependence has moved beyond the fear of rejection, for she knows that others need her as much as she needs them.

I like what the Buddhist monk and author Thich Nhat Hanh has to say about interdependence. Hanh asks his audiences to hold a piece of paper in their hands and to consider it carefully. Then he tells them, "The whole world is in this piece of paper."

When you consider the piece of paper these very words are written upon, you too must consider the entire world. The paper exists because of the tree from which it came, because of the logger who fell the tree, because of the farmer who raised the food that fed the logger, because of the mill that pressed the wood into paper, because of the steel that makes the mill, because of the cotton that clothes the mill worker, and on it goes. Eventually, you are forced to consider the ultimate interdependence of everything in the entire universe.

The fear of rejection says: "Your gift of approval is more important than my gift of self." Interdependence says: "I offer my gifts to you and you offer your gifts to me; neither gift is better or worse, more or less important." Interdependence honors the sanctity of every human and the value of his or her talents.

Irrational Belief #2: Other people's opinions define me.

Maybe this belief is better stated as: "What will the neighbors think?" After all, that's what so many of us heard as children, and it is the essence of the irrational belief. Ultimately, what another person thinks about you and your talents has no relevance to the worth of your efforts. Perhaps that person doesn't need what you have to offer, but that is in no way saying that what you have to offer isn't valuable.

This is a hard lesson I had to learn when I first started writing and publishing my books. At the start of the process, the usual routine is to prepare a short proposal and send it out to many editors. The editors then bid on the proposal if they would like to publish it. When I first started writing proposals and sending them out, I would get responses that were all over the board. Some editors liked my ideas and would place a bid on the book I was proposing; others either didn't bother to respond or sent back some cryptic message saying they didn't think the project was worthwhile.

I eventually learned that some of the biggest successes in publishing history initially were unable to find a publisher. In fact, one of the best-selling books of all time, *Chicken Soup for the Soul*, was rejected more than a dozen times before Health Communications, a relatively unknown publisher at the time, decided to publish it.

What I discovered about my own work was that success was as much about finding the people who respond to my work as it is about the quality of what I do. If someone doesn't care for my work, that's fine—there are others who will.

If you allow the opinions of others, particularly the criticisms, to define you and your work, you will never succeed. It doesn't matter what you do or how well you do it; someone will find fault with it. When you internalize all of that negative information, you will eventually lose all confidence in your talents.

Step 2: Make a conscious effort to push past the fear even though you continue to feel it.

The best way to overcome the fear of rejection is to look those who you fear will reject you straight in the eye. Why? Most often, those who we fear will reject us are those people we keep at a distance. Because we have limited our exposure to them, we ascribe all kinds of qualities to them that they may not have. Get close to those you think might reject you and learn as much as you can about them. Every time I have an executive do this, the result is the same: she discovers that the other person is human, too, and nothing to be afraid of. Of course, it can be nerve-racking to be around those powerful others who can influence your present job, but when you do it, you will begin to sense the fear diminish.

As with all fears, fearing rejection creates a behavior cycle that actually elicits rejection from others. We expect that others will reject us, and as a result we either push them away or cling to them; actions that usually drive them away from us. In order to break the cycle of fear, we must push through the feeling and learn to trust others—even when we worry that they might reject our trust.

In Chapter 2, I mentioned the executive named Susan who so feared rejection that she ultimately alienated herself from her staff. Susan could have broken the cycle of fear by trusting her staff to do their work without having to examine everything they did. Even when she worried that they might betray her, she could have continued trusting the employees until she had solid, factual evidence that they were behaving otherwise. The simple act of trusting those staff members would have been a powerful message that would have elicited loyalty from her staff, even if they had originally intended to undermine her. It is extraordinarily difficult for even the hardest of individuals to undermine someone who trusts them.

Step 3: Take positive action in the direction of your fear.

Identify those people in your life whom you want to impress. Write down a list. Now, next to each name, write down something about yourself that you've gone out of your way to hide from that person. Over the next few weeks, make a plan to reveal that part of yourself to the person you want to impress.

As you do this, two things will happen. First, you will discover not only that most people will appreciate the authenticity, but that your action will improve your relationship. Second, you will discover that the freedom and relief you feel is far more valuable than anything you might have gotten from that person had you been able to impress them. If they choose to reject you for who you are, is that your fault? That's valuable information for you because it tells you that maybe it's time to move on and find another place where your talents are needed and appreciated.

Breaking the fear of rejection does not mean that you will stop enjoying the approval of others. It is to say, however, that the approval of others is no longer a driving force in your life and career. To the extent that others accept you as you are, you form healthy and mutually satisfying relationships.

However, when others accept you only if you conform to their expectations, then you must be willing to live without that acceptance. To be your best, your need for approval must be subordinate to the expression of your talents.

Ironically, when you value your talents over the approval of others it earns their sincere respect. Even when they disagree with you, they respect the fact that you are staying true to yourself and are acting upon your own values. This kind of acceptance—based solely on integrity—is the only satisfying form of acceptance.

Every successful executive has, at one time or another, struggled with the fear of rejection. The tug of organizational membership is so strong that it is easy for us to lose our perspective and trade ourselves for acceptance and approval. Perhaps you even work in an organization that thrives on the threat of rejection: "He's not a team player" is sometimes a euphemism for "He's unwilling to compromise himself as we have done." Engaging in this fear, however, is something your successful career can't afford.

NOTES

1. Charles W. Eliot, ed., *The Harvard Classics: FolkLore and Fable: Aesop, Grimm, Andersen* (New York: P. F. Collier & Son, 1909).
2. Irving L. Janis, *Groupthink* (Boston: Houghton Mifflin, 1982).
3. Daniel Ellsberg, "The Quagmire Myth and the Stalemate Machine." *Public Policy*, Spring 1971.
4. Ibid.
5. Ibid.
6. H. Sidey, "White House Staff vs. The Cabinet." *Washington Monthly*, February 1969.
7. I. Graff, *The Tuesday Cabinet* (Englewood Cliffs, NJ: Prentice-Hall, 1970).
8. Andrew Grove. "Taking the Hype Out of Leadership." *Fortune*, March 28, 1988.

FIVE

Fear of Scarcity: What If Someone Else Steals My Piece of the Action?

In 1985, Carl Icahn bought a controlling stake in TWA, at the time one of the country's strongest airlines. TWA owned the prized New York-to-London and Chicago-to-London routes, as well as a host of other profitable domestic routes. Icahn, a notorious corporate raider, had a history of running businesses on extraordinarily tight budgets, and he applied this philosophy with vigor to TWA.

During Icahn's tenure at TWA he failed to update the aircraft fleet, making TWA's the oldest in the country. In addition, he demanded that employees take a 22 percent pay cut at a time when other airlines were giving out raises, which created substantial labor relations difficulties between the airline and the unions. And those prized London routes? Icahn sold them to Delta.

Today, TWA still bears the scars of Icahn's tenure. The airline has struggled in recent years on the verge of bankruptcy. Though it was once among the top three airlines, it now ranks toward the bottom of the list.

What Icahn's management style shows is a clear fear of scarcity. It is a model that is based on limiting resources and cutting costs to attain profitability. In a mammoth study on the subject, Mercer Management, an international management consulting company, examined more than one thousand companies and discovered that only 7 percent of the best performing companies had cut costs during the previous five years.[1]

Let me be quick to say that cutting unnecessary expenses is a legitimate and effective way to restore profitability to a financially ailing company. Cutting expenses, however, *is not a business plan*. It is a reaction to current difficult circumstances, and cannot successfully maintain a company in the long run.

There is a fine line between accurately assessing decreases in revenue and running scared of imagined scarcity. When the latter happens, executives have crossed the line into the fear that tells them there aren't enough resources for success. This executive who fears scarcity is slow to take risks, so slow that she often misses great opportunities for growth. She is looking for a sure thing—something that simply doesn't exist. Every business deal has risk, and some of the most profitable ones carry the greater risk. She is chasing a fantasy.

The fear of scarcity is often a very personal fear for the executive who extends beyond just management practices. This executive is unconsciously afraid that her life will come to a place of pain and needless suffering, and that she won't have enough of the things that make living possible or worthwhile. She fears the scarcity of money, food, shelter, companionship, love, challenge, and respect.

When you entertain this idea, you too are participating in the fear of scarcity. You have lost faith in the inherent wisdom of your talents. Perhaps the natural course of events will land you in the gutter, hungry and lost. For most of us, this fear is entirely imagined and irrational. What do we really need in order to live? To be fulfilled? The answer is that we need far less than what most of us have today. Yet, we imagine that we might be forced to go without and that such a lack would be very painful.

As you engage the fear of scarcity, you convince yourself that you must hold on to what you have today and protect yourself from the imagined disasters that change might bring. You stockpile and insure, thinking that without a hedge, your demise will surely occur.

STOP! DON'T CHANGE

The fear of scarcity leads to one of two reactions, the first being to *stop change*. Rather than allowing ourselves to unfold naturally, according to the wisdom of our talents, we seize upon the success of today, doing everything we can to keep it within our reach. We tell ourselves that the key to our survival is maintaining our current state and eliminating risk from our lives. But even in the palm of our clinched fist, change continues to occur. Life marches onward, regardless of our protests. It is the way of the universe.

An Old Slice

A few years ago, there was a remarkable illustration of how far some will go to stop change and hold on to the past. On February 19, 1998, a piece of cake was auctioned off at Sotheby's in New York for $29,000. It wasn't just any piece of cake, as you might imagine; it was a boxed piece of wedding cake from the 1937 marriage of the Duke and Duchess of Windsor. Even more amazing, all that was left in the box tied with white ribbon was some residual cake dust.

For an entire generation, the Duke and Duchess of Windsor were the epitome of romance. After the death of his father, King George V, in 1936, the Duke was crowned King Edward VIII. However, his love for Mrs. Wallis Simpson, a divorced American, was stronger than his desire to be king, and so he abdicated the throne to marry her. For the rest of their lives, the former king and his bride lived together in virtual exile from England.

So it was that a symbol of their love—a piece of wedding cake—caused quite a stir. Sotheby's had underestimated that excitement, putting a value on the small box of cake at less than $1,000. But when it came to the auctioneer's podium, the bidding was fierce, and when it finally sold, the well-heeled crowd couldn't contain themselves and erupted into applause.

Despite the treasured memories surrounding the now disintegrated wedding cake, it, like everything else, has changed. Nothing is permanent; all is in flux. No matter how much we want something to stay constant, it will not. Our attempts to stop change become prisons of our own making. As the fear grows, we expend more and more effort trying to stop the unstoppable. We set limits on ourselves, refusing to encounter risk. As a result, we slowly diminish our efficacy.

The executive who becomes entangled in the fear of scarcity, in the words of management jargon, sits down on the job. The stance of this executive moves from the offensive to the defensive. He holds on to his job, taking the path of least resistance, hoping to maintain the success he has attained. But the truth is that every executive, regardless of the company, is either moving "up or out," growing, or dying. There is no treading water. There is no standing still. If we are not risking, pushing, or growing, then we are slowly diminishing.

The only true hedge you have against scarcity is to grow according to your talents. In the economy of life, you must continually make investments of reasonable risk to stay ahead of the inflation of change. If you fail to do this and try to hide your assets under the mattress, it is only a matter of time before change overtakes you and renders your hidden treasure worthless. Assets are only valuable when they are working for you.

NEEDY, GREEDY, GRABBY

The other reaction to the fear of scarcity is one of competitive greed. We become convinced that we aren't getting our fair share—that someone else is stealing what is rightfully ours. Life becomes a zero-sum game, where the only way to win is to force our opponent to lose.

This kind of competition among executives not only destroys careers, it can also destroy the company. Your fear of scarcity becomes focused on your peers. If they appear to do better than you, you assume that you are somehow diminished, and you are then motivated to attack their success. Rather than making decisions for the common good of the company, you selectively act to benefit yourself and to diminish your peers.

This is classic corporate politics, and it is fueled by the fear of scarcity. Rather than viewing corporate success as a potentially ever-increasing pie (where all slices grow larger together), we choose to see it as a dish of finite dimension, where a bigger portion for me means a smaller piece for you.

STEVE JOBS

It was in the fall of 1983 when I first encountered the "Lisa." Lisa, an Apple computer, was the most fascinating, easy-to-use computer I had ever seen. With just a click of a button she could rearrange paragraphs of text or insert words into a sentence. She could do footnotes, table of contents, indexes, and bibliographies with a few simple commands. Simple things, like switching from single-spaced to double-spaced text could be done in a second, something that previously had required retyping the entire manuscript. Fascinated, I must have sat for more than an hour peering in the green phosphorous monitor and watching the salesperson move the strange-looking mouse as images danced across Lisa's screen.

Looking back, I realize how fortunate I was that the Lisa was out of reach for my pocketbook. It was discontinued after six months and very few of them were made. Precious little software had been written for the computer, and the little that was written wasn't compatible with any other personal computer, Apple or otherwise. Although the press gushed over the Lisa's user-friendly, icon-driven display and praised her ability to do complex tasks, her rise and fall happened with unparalleled speed. Although very few knew it at the time, the world had witnessed in the Lisa the fallout of an internal corporate competitive struggle.

Steve Jobs, one-time whiz kid of the computer industry, was the creative talent behind Apple Computers. Much to his credit, he cultivated the company from a small, mail-order business in a garage to the internationally known entity it is today. The Lisa computer, named after his own daughter, was his prized project. When he became embroiled in a heated political battle at Apple, he also became a major force in the Lisa's demise.

Promoted and fueled by Steve, the Lisa project team became something of an elitist club within Apple, which garnered the resentment of the other divisions. To begin with, you had to have and wear a special bright orange badge to even be admitted into the building that housed the Lisa team. Further, Steve had hired many well-trained, professional programmers to work on the project, not the typical young, do-it-by-your-instincts hackers that had traditionally populated Apple. Apple had always hired passionate amateurs who never outlined a program before writing, who never wasted time on theoretical models, and who thought that, for the most part, program comments were "for sissies."

Tensions at Apple began to rise and morale started to

plummet as Steve spoke disparagingly of the Apple II division to anyone who would listen. He referred to it as "the dull and boring product division" at a time when the Apple II was extremely profitable and was financing the rest of the company—including Steve's precious Lisa. He even told the press that the Lisa would "leave the Apple II in the dust."

The rest of Apple senior management, aware of this conflict, met unbeknownst to Steve to reorganize the company. The net result of the reorganization approved by the board of directors was that Steve was removed from any formal operating position. The Lisa project was given to another manager, John Couch. Shocked by the announcement, Steve was bitter at not having been consulted. He felt betrayed and his ego was badly bruised.

Recovering only in appearance from the Lisa fiasco, Steve moved on in the following months to another project, the little brother to Lisa, known as Macintosh. Now more politically savvy, Steve had learned some hard lessons from the Lisa experience and was determined not to make the same mistakes with the Macintosh.

Steve located his hand-picked Macintosh design team in a building several miles from the rest of the Apple divisions, where he alone decided layout and office assignments. There he created the ultimate post-teenage work environment for the young programmers. A stereo with speakers that were six feet high was installed in the offices and a Japanese masseur was placed on call for anyone in the group who worked late— all paid for by the company. The Macintosh refrigerator was stocked with fresh juices and mineral waters at a cost of $100,000 a year. As a larger-than-life reminder of his expectations of excellence, he placed a $50,000 Bossendorfer grand piano in the lobby of the office. The parking lot at the Texaco towers, the nickname of the building where the team was located, was filled with expensive European cars like BMWs and Saabs, which Steve had arranged for the company to lease on behalf of the team. Whenever anyone from the Macintosh team flew on company business, they traveled first class, even when their other Apple employees were flying coach on the same trip.

When the time came to roll out the Lisa, Macintosh was still six months away from introduction. Steve made the trip to New York for the unveiling of the Lisa, and filled a $575-a-night suite at the Hotel Carlyle with a team of both Lisa and Apple managers, who had worked together on the plan to unveil the machine before the press. It was Apple's first attempt at an orchestrated product introduction, and it was Steve's chance to shine.

Surprisingly, while introducing the revolutionary new Lisa to the media, Steve began describing not the Lisa, but the Macintosh. *Business Week* quoted Steve as saying "when it comes out, Mac is going to be the most incredible computer in the world—another Apple II."[2] He proudly described the Mac's features as "like Lisa" but at one quarter of the $10,000 Lisa price tag. With one fell stroke, he turned the fascination and awe over Lisa into wait-and-see anticipation for the not yet completed Macintosh. It's not surprising that buyers eagerly waited to see what was coming before investing in the Lisa, a reaction that killed the computer before it was ever really launched. The final kiss of death for Lisa was the surprising announcement that the Macintosh and Lisa would not be compatible, which meant if an office bought a Lisa, the files and programs could not be transferred to a Macintosh that might be purchased in the future.

Jobs' fear of scarcity had convinced him that the only way the Macintosh would succeed was by stealing customers from the Lisa. Rather than imagining a growing market—one that had ample customers for both the powerful Lisa and the more portable Macintosh—Jobs acted as though the market had a limited and finite set of customers who would buy only one or the other.

Ironically, if there has been any lesson learned from the personal computer revolution, it is that no market is ever truly mature or truly limited. Just when you think sales have leveled, a new feature on a product opens the floodgate to a new source of sales.

IT'S PERSONAL, TOO

The fear of scarcity is something that dogs executives in both their careers and personal lives. For example, Stan, whom I've known for more than fifteen years, is a likable, well-read fellow who has a wicked sense of humor. Stan has worked in his family's furniture business for most of his life and recently retired to Florida. When he was young, his father, who had lived through the Great Depression, opened a furniture store. His father's memories of the Depression were so strong he lived most of his life as if hard times were always just around the corner. He saved every nickel he could squeeze from his business. His store was always sparse and the furniture he sold was no frills and very functional.

Through his father's strong influence, Stan grew up with similar ideas. Even though the business had been successful for many years after his father's death, Stan ran it on a shoe-string, amassing a great deal of cash in the bank. There was a very dark side to Stan's frugality. He would go to any length to save a dime. He never paid his employees very well; as a result, the good ones usually moved over to his better-paying competitors after a few years of working for him, which only further fueled his suspicions. In his personal life, Stan was never able to maintain a romantic relationship for long. His first marriage ended in divorce, largely because Stan con-stantly berated his wife for spending too much. Other rela-tionships came and went in a similar fashion. By the time Stan was in his mid-50s, he refused to date women because he felt they would only want him for his money.

When Stan retired to Florida, he put his home in Virginia on the market. It was a large house he had purchased many years before. At the time he bought the house, the neighbor-hood was quite run-down, and he had picked up the house for a mere pittance. In the decades following, the neighbor-hood was restored, and the houses were now among the most expensive in town. By the time Stan retired, the house was worth more than six times what he originally paid for it.

Of course, this wasn't enough for Stan. He put the house on the market for an outrageous price, all the time maintain-ing that he wasn't going to "give it away." And since owning a house both in Florida and Virginia seemed wildly extrava-gant, Stan rented a very small efficiency apartment in Florida, where he has lived for the past two years. The apartment is unbelievably cramped and piled to the ceiling with old furni-ture and other stuff Stan refuses to part with.

Rather than put a fair price on the house in Virginia so it

will sell, Stan refuses to budge and continues to pay some rather hefty maintenance fees to keep the yard mowed and the house in good condition. Even though he has more than enough money to live very comfortably throughout his retirement in Florida, Stan chooses to horde his money and stay in his small apartment, all the time complaining bitterly about the close quarters.

Stan is an example of the extremes to which the fear of scarcity can drive you. This fear makes you a slave to your possessions. You become convinced that some dark calamity will happen if you don't stockpile as a protection against imagined disaster. Like Stan, you stay miserable in jobs you hate simply because you fear that you might not have enough to survive otherwise. You avoid all risk and work like a dog to accumulate what you mistakenly believe will make you happy.

The fear of scarcity limits your thinking, and ultimately hurts you. In the case of Apple Computers, Steve Jobs was a major shareholder at the time of the Lisa introduction. Hence, his battle against the Lisa not only hurt company revenues, it hurt his personal finances. Similarly, under the influence of the fear of scarcity, you too can fail to see how helping the larger organization succeed increases everyone's share of the profit, including your own. Ultimately, you hurt yourself by creating the scarcity you are trying to avoid.

Breaking the Cycle of Fear

Step 1: Acknowledge and confront the irrational beliefs that underlie your fear of scarcity.

Irrational Belief #1: The universe of possibilities is finite.

Nothing is completely finite. Sure, there are certain limits to everything, but within and around those limitations are infinite possibilities. There is not just *one* way to make a business more profitable, nor is there only *one* way to close a lucrative deal. The possibilities are only limited by our outlook.

Nothing is truly finite; we only see it that way. Sure, you may run out of a particular resource, but there is always another resource that can be substituted. For example, I once had a home on a small island where there was no more land available for new buildings. If you were a builder there, you might have thought that your business would die, right? Not so. Building contractors on that island thrived as they bought older structures, tore them down, and built multilevel buildings. If newcomers to the island couldn't find a house they liked, they would often purchase an existing home, tear it down, and build what they wanted. The shortage of land only led to new ways of building multifamily dwellings.

The same is true with almost everything in business. Unfortunately, the fear of scarcity leads you to believe that resources are finite and that you must get as much as possible if you want to be successful. Rather than creating new streams of revenue, you focus on protecting what you have. While that might be successful in the short run, it will always hurt your career in the long term. Eventually a competitor will hit the same "limit" that you have reached and find another way around it. All sustainable business success is based on one principle: growth. Hoarding, cutting, and saving may be appropriate for a short-term crisis, but those actions will never achieve long-term success.

When you choose to believe that the universe of possibilities is exhausted, you limit yourself and your success. Ultimately that type of thinking will cause you to decide that the world already has enough of what you have to offer. So why try? Focusing on limits is in itself career limiting.

Irrational Belief #2: How much I own is the measure of my success.

A large number of executives believe that their success is measured by how much they own. Not surprisingly, that puts them on the career treadmill of trying to make ever-increasing salaries.

It is alarming how many wealthy executives approaching retirement are incredibly dissatisfied and unfulfilled by their careers. Much of their disappointment has to do with the faulty belief that wealth is the measure of success. Wealth certainly helps one to be comfortable and secure, but it isn't success and it doesn't satisfy the cravings of the executive soul. The majority of executives with whom I work, both young and old, have a strong desire to make a difference in the world. They want to accomplish something that has meaning to them—not just hold a job. Sadly, some mistakenly believe that making large sums of money will satisfy that urge, and when it doesn't, they become disillusioned and somewhat bitter about their careers.

On the other hand, those who have relentlessly followed their passion and accomplished something they felt was meaningful are by far the happiest and most enjoyable executives with whom I work. Regardless of whether or not they have made a fortune (and some have done quite well), they are fulfilled. They can't imagine having spent their lives doing anything other than what they do.

Following your dream is the only measure of success that will really satisfy your soul. Even if that dream leads you through multiple failures, *it is a life you have created.* That, and only that, is the true measure of success.

Step 2: Make a conscious effort to push past the fear even though you continue to feel it.

The feeling of the fear of scarcity often comes in the form of anxiety about another person's success. When you see one of your peers succeeding, you start to quietly panic, thinking that somehow their success has diminished yours. The fear can also manifest itself in the feeling of anxiety about another executive's failure. You watched as that executive took a risk and failed, and you determine that you won't make the same mistake; thus, you stop taking risks.

When either of these feelings arise, remind yourself that the only true success in life comes from practicing your talents. The more you do it, the more successful you become, regardless of what you own. Remember that *success is nothing more than a feeling.* It is the feeling of having accomplished something that is worthwhile to you. So even when others around you are receiving more accolades or, conversely, failing, you can remain secure in your own success. You are creating the career that is perfect for you.

Step 3: Take positive action in the direction of your fear.

Eliminating the fear of scarcity in our lives requires a return to one principal belief: *I am sufficient.* You already have everything you need to survive and accomplish your highest potential. Until you embrace this belief and hold it within the core of your being, you will continually be fighting for survival. No matter what success or wealth comes your way, it will never be enough. You will never be free to enjoy the bounty of your labor, for you will continually be fighting a war against scarcity.

The fear of scarcity plays on the belief that you are not sufficient. It supposes there are threats to your well-being all around you and you must continually be about the business of avoiding and conquering. If you are not successful, horrible things will happen.

Ironically, it is the belief in personal insufficiency that creates that reality. When you imagine yourself as weak and vulnerable, that is your perception, and hence, your experience. By believing in your own lack, you create that lack around yourself. You do and say things that communicate your fear of scarcity, and others with whom you do business pick up on it. They, in turn, react to your fear and move away from you. Consequently, your own lack of belief in yourself fulfills itself and creates scarcity.

When you believe in yourself and trust your talents, you act confidently. Others are attracted to you and they help make your positive beliefs a reality. It is a fundamental law of human behavior: people are attracted to others' confidence and are motivated to help create their success.

By refusing to believe in scarcity, you actually free yourself from its control. When you trust your talent to provide you with all the tools you need for success, you no longer worry about insufficiency and lack. You know there is no situation that comes your way that you cannot handle. Hence, there is no reason to fear.

NOTES

1. John Micklethwait and Adrian Wooldridge, *The Witch Doctors: Making Sense of the Management Gurus* (New York: Times Business, 1996).
2. *Business Week*, 31 January 1983.

SIX

Fear of Reality: Isn't There a Quick Fix?

CALLING 911

Imagine if you could call 911 from your office and hear the following: "Thank you for calling the management emergency hotline. For declining revenue, press 1. For out-of-control expenses, press 2. For employee morale problems, press 3. For an unresponsive senior management, press 4. For all other problems, stay on the line and someone will help you right away."

Of course, you can't make such a call. Or can you? Since the early 1980s, corporations have increasingly come to depend on management consultants. And not a few companies use consultants like a management emergency line. Whenever they need a quick fix, they call the consultant. American businesses now spend a whopping $15 billion a year on outside advice—and that figure is growing rapidly every year. One of the leading management consulting "gurus" charges $60,000 for a one-day session, and remarkably, he books more than sixty of these engagements per year.[1]

There's nothing wrong with calling in the experts, particularly when you don't have certain expertise in-house, but the phenomenal growth in the management guru industry is clearly not due to the occasional expert intervention in company affairs. By all accounts, including those of highly paid consultants, this growth has come about because some executives have become enamored with the idea of a magical solution and, simultaneously, have lost confidence in their own management abilities.

Modern business reality is very tough. There is little room for learning by trial and error, and the consequences of failure can be brutal and inhumane. It's understandable that so many executives try to escape this reality by hiring consultants and other prepackaged problem solvers to magically make it all OK. The problem is there is no magical solution.

THE GREAT ESCAPE

When you encounter problems that are so daunting that they threaten to overtake your business, you must take action. But what to do? You've been working hard, doing everything you know to do, and suddenly this seemingly insurmountable situation arises. It is not only threatening to your business interests, it also poses a threat to the viability of your judgment. To put it bluntly: Your best thinking got you here and where you are ain't too pretty.

That's when you need some magic. You need something you haven't tried before, something that in better times you might not have considered, but now you're ready for anything that promises a cure. You start shopping for gurus, doctors, and corporate evangelists.

Certainly, much good is transacted between the advice givers and their clients, but there is a more troubling issue in the dramatically rising trend of purchasing outside expertise. Quick fixes and fads abound. Much that is old hat is being relabeled and sold under new guises. Increasingly, executives are willing to trade off their own judgment for that of an expert who supposedly knows more about the problem and its solution. By hiring an expert to solve a problem, you can scratch it off your to-do list. Done—the problem has been taken care of. Let the experts handle it. Now you're off the hook and can move on to the next issue.

This is really an escape from a reality that you'd rather not deal with. Instead of grappling with the real issues, like "What have I done to create this problem?" or "It may take years of hard work to overcome this difficulty," you prefer to hand it over to someone else who promises a quick and painless fix.

Ask any business consultant and he or she will tell you that many clients don't want to hear the unwashed truth about their business. Instead, they want to hear what remarkable thing the consultant will do to make the business wildly successful. Rather than hearing about changes in their behavior or the need for personal involvement and commitment to change, they want to hear about the process or program that will magically transform this current lackluster reality into stellar performance.

The escape from reality and the search for gurus is a timeless experience. Through the ages there have been countless stories of people from all cultures seeking to find some magic that they didn't already possess. One of these stories, *The Wizard of Oz,* by L. Frank Baum, was immortalized in an early Technicolor motion picture and is beloved by children all around the world.

The Wizard and the Emerald City

In the familiar story of Dorothy and the Wizard of Oz, the young Dorothy is caught in a cyclone that takes her far away from her family in Kansas. When she awakens, she discovers that she is in the magical land of Oz, which is ruled by the good Wizard. Much to her distress, she discovers that the only person who can get her back to Kansas is the Wizard, who lives in the faraway Emerald City.

So Dorothy begins a pilgrimage down the yellow brick road that leads to the Emerald City. Along the way, she meets several traveling partners: the Scarecrow, the Tin Woodman, and the Cowardly Lion. Each of them decides to travel to the Wizard so that he can give them something they want: The Scarecrow wants brains; the Tin Woodman wants a heart; and the Cowardly Lion wants courage.

After a number of encounters along the way, all four make it to the great gate of the Emerald City, only to discover that the Wizard will grant their wishes only AFTER they have killed the Wicked Witch of the West and returned with her broom. So, off they go to find the Witch and retrieve her broom, which they finally achieve after a great deal of intrigue.

Upon returning with the broom, however, they discover the Wizard to be a fake—nothing more than a small, bald man from Omaha who has fooled the entire kingdom of Oz with his charade of being a Wizard. Although the Wizard has no magical powers, he tells the foursome to return to him the next morning and he will grant their wishes.

In the chapter titled "The Magic Art of the Great Humbug," Baum writes:

> Next morning the Scarecrow said to his friends:
>
> "Congratulate me. I am going to Oz to get my brains at last. When I return I shall be as other men are."
>
> "I have always liked you as you were," said Dorothy simply.
>
> "It is kind of you to like a Scarecrow," he replied. "But surely you will think more of me when you hear the splendid thoughts my new brain is going to turn out." Then he said good-bye to them all in a cheerful voice and went to the Throne Room, where he rapped upon the door.
>
> "Come in," said Oz.
>
> The Scarecrow went in and found the little man sitting down by the window, engaged in deep thought.
>
> "I have come for my brains," remarked the Scarecrow, a little uneasily.
>
> "Oh, yes; sit down in that chair, please," replied Oz. "You must excuse me for taking your head off, but I shall have to do it in order to put your brains in their proper place."
>
> "That's all right," said the Scarecrow. "You are quite welcome to take my head off as long as it will be a better one when you put it on again."
>
> So the Wizard unfastened his head and emptied out the straw. Then he entered the back room and took up a measure of bran, which he mixed with a great many pins and needles. Having shaken them together thoroughly, he filled the top of the Scarecrow's head with the mixture and stuffed the rest of the space with straw, to hold it in place.
>
> When he had fastened the Scarecrow's head on his body again he said to him, "Hereafter you will be a great man, for I have given you a lot of bran-new brains."

The Scarecrow was both pleased and proud at the fulfillment of his greatest wish, and having thanked Oz warmly he went back to his friends.

Dorothy looked at him curiously. His head was quite bulged out at the top with brains.

"How do you feel?" she asked.

"I feel wise indeed," he answered earnestly. "When I get used to my brains I shall know everything."

"Why are those needles and pins sticking out of your head?" asked the Tin Woodman.

"That is proof that he is sharp," remarked the Lion.[2]

And so the story goes, as the Wizard convinces the Scarecrow, the Lion, and the Woodman that they now have the magical solutions they were seeking. With a shocking similarity to the private conversations of modern management consultants, the Wizard said: "How can I help being a humbug when all these people make me do things that everybody knows can't be done? It was easy to make the Scarecrow and the Lion and the Woodman happy, because they imagined I could do anything."[3]

Of course, the Wizard wasn't able to give the Scarecrow, the Lion, or the Woodman what they sought, but what he did give them was the knowledge that what they wanted was inside themselves all along. After having conquered the Wicked Witch, the Lion found out he already had courage; the Woodman found his heart in the feelings he had for Dorothy and the other companions; and the Scarecrow discovered he had all the smarts he needed to survive.

It wasn't the Wizard who gave them what they needed— it was the confidence they learned in themselves throughout their difficult journey that did the trick. The Wizard only symbolized that for them with his gifts.

Perhaps this seems a bit simple to you, but I find it enormously profound (as most profundities are painfully simple). Just like those wacky characters in Baum's story, the executive who fears reality also seeks magical relief. The only true relief lies within ourselves, and the best gurus (and management consultants) teach us this. They help us to find the confidence within ourselves to solve the problems that face us. They have no magical fixes, shortcuts, or processes that we don't already have. All they can do is point us to the talents within ourselves. *Your talent is all the magic you will ever need.*

THE MAGIC WORD

Another way in which executives are seduced by the fear of reality is by believing that simply naming a problem will solve it. Words like "reengineering," "rightsizing," and "decommitting" (my all-time favorite; it means to stop committing resources to a project and usually entails layoffs) are labels that we hang upon complex problems within the organization. We fool ourselves into thinking that if we can put a word on the problem, draw a box around it, and fit it on an overhead slide then it is solved. Most of the time, however, we've only lulled ourselves with a false sense of accomplishment. Naming a problem doesn't solve it.

The same is true with real solutions—naming the solution isn't the same as implementing it. I remember working in a large high-tech company back in the late 1980s when two technologies were just blooming. They were "distributed data processing" and "RISC (reduced instruction set chip) technology." Although very few of the employees or managers really understood these technologies or what they meant to the company, everyone was using the words to describe future plans. They became magical words that when uttered, heads nodded in agreement (almost as if someone had said "hocus-pocus"). We weren't exactly sure what these things were, but we knew they were good and would be the way of the future.

SHORTCUTS

Still another way in which we avoid reality is a relentless belief in shortcuts. There must be some way to accomplish a mundane task with greatly reduced time and effort. Rarely, if ever, do these shortcuts exist. More times than not, the supposed "shortcut" takes more time and resources than doing the job thoroughly the first time.

Remember the first personal computer that landed on your office desk? These new machines were sold to executives at all levels of the company as "shortcuts" to work. They were going to magically reduce the amount of time and effort most people were required to expend on their jobs—and better yet, eliminate most office paperwork. With just the push of a button we were going to have all the information we needed to do our jobs.

Without a doubt, computers have improved our lives, but it is doubtful, even many years later, that personal computers have created enormously helpful "shortcuts." In fact, most people's experience with the machines is that they require a great deal of time in training and maintenance, not to mention the sizable cost of software programs and technical support. Gains in efficiency and productivity as the result of personal computers have come slowly and with a sizable price tag. So it is with all increases in efficiency—they come in small, painfully earned steps.

Nevertheless, you continue to search for a magic bullet that will solve your problems. New technology, while it holds great promise, has rarely produced shortcuts. Most often, it simply helps you to do what you already know how to do— and if you're lucky, to do it a bit faster or more easily.

Particularly when it comes to people, there are no shortcuts. Customers still want the personal touch, and clients still like to be contacted in person—regardless of the telephone routing system or the automated teller. Employees still need time to assimilate change, no matter how quickly the market shifts. And senior management still likes to eyeball the troops. As long as we are human, I'm betting that not much of this will change.

BREAKING THE CYCLE OF FEAR

Step 1: Acknowledge and confront the irrational beliefs that underlie your fear of reality.

Irrational Belief #1: Appearances are all that matter.

Ever been involved in a corporate cover-up? Most executives have had that experience at one time or another, and some have actually built their careers on dressing up problems in order to hide them. Rather than admit that a program has failed, they dress up a failure to make it look like a success.

The root of this problem is best described in a statement one executive made to me: "Perception is all that matters." In other words, it doesn't really matter what the truth is as long as the perception of it is good. As long as the window dressing is good, who cares about the truth? Not much is happening to solve the real problem.

Consultants are often major players in this area. A management team that is running scared of reality will often call in a consulting firm to study the situation, not because the executives don't know what's wrong, but because they need to look like they are doing something to solve the problem. In these situations, it's not uncommon that every employee, from top executives down to the mailroom staff, knows what the organization's problems are. The issue is that the executives are afraid of what it will take to fix the problems. Instead of facing this fear, they stall by initiating lengthy studies by well-known experts. The perception is that something is being done to solve the problem, while the reality is that the problem is only growing worse.

I once consulted for a retail company that operates small boutique-type stores in strip malls across the country. The executive in charge of the stores knew what was causing a severe drop in sales, but was terrified to engage a solution. The problem was that the store interiors were dated—they looked like something from the 1970s, with dark colors and bright fluorescent lights. The stores looked tired, and the dark colors made them look unclean compared to the newer, pastel interiors and softer lighting of the competitors. But with more than a thousand stores nationwide, remodeling all the stores would take a major injection of capital and more than five years to complete.

The executive with whom I worked engaged the services of a well-respected consulting firm to study the problem. When the consultants came back with a recommendation to remodel the stores, he terminated the engagement and discarded the report. In the meantime, he continued to tinker with minor changes in the display units of a few of the stores, and predictably, this had no impact on sales. He used that information as evidence that it wasn't the store interiors or fixtures that were the problem, and he then proceeded to place the blame on everything from the product mix to the training of the sales associates.

What is really interesting about this case is that everyone—and I do mean *everyone*, including the executive—knew that the store interiors were a problem. Every year that passed, though, the problem had grown worse as the stores began to look even shabbier. Eventually, the problem was denied for so long the solution was extremely costly and the executive didn't want to be responsible for the bad news. He covered up the truth long enough to land a job at another company, which he did. When the company finally dealt with the problem, the remodeling costs caused the company to be unprofitable for more than two years.

The irrational belief that you can solve a problem by hiding it is a form of denial that only makes the real problem grow worse. Eventually, you have to pay the piper and when you do, it is often a far greater cost than what you tried to avoid in the first place.

Irrational Belief #2: Success is a matter of luck.

When you believe that success is a matter of luck, your only task is to do what you can to get lucky. So you move from job to job, hoping that your luck will improve. You see other executives "getting lucky" and you wonder why it hasn't happened for you.

While this may sound a bit pathetic, think about it carefully. A surprising number of well-educated, aspiring executives hold this belief. Rather than committing themselves to the hard work that success almost always takes, they spend their time and energy looking for a lucky situation. Since difficult situations appear to be rather unlucky, they avoid such places and look for those that will enhance their career.

Unfortunately for such executives, every business encounters difficult situations. Not one organization or executive is exempt. What makes most businesses successful is how well they navigate troubled waters. Executives who are trying to get lucky must jump ship when things get rough. As a result, their luck never seems to change for the better. The truth is that successful executives create their own luck.

Irrational Belief #3: Pain should always be avoided.

Nobody likes to be in pain, but everyone is from time to time. Pain isn't a sign of failure, it's a sign of a problem that needs to be fixed—and there is a big difference between the two. When the executive sees pain as a failure, she is strongly motivated to escape the pain.

In Chapter 2, I told the story of Susan, an executive who abruptly quit after getting a mediocre performance review. Susan's behavior is also reflective of the avoidance of pain. Of course, nobody likes to receive a negative review, but the point of such a review is to bring about change, not avoidance. Had Susan chosen to stay, it would have taken a swallowing of pride and a renewed commitment to buckle down and work hard, all of which would have transformed the pain of the review into something positive for her career. Instead, she chose to leave, destroying her relationship with the organization and putting something of a negative mark on her résumé. By avoiding the pain, she actually hurt herself even more.

Step 2: Make a conscious effort to push past the fear even though you continue to feel it.

If you are to be an effective executive, you must be continually thinking about the business of engaging reality, not avoiding it with wishful thinking. Confronting the true complexities of today's business problems, rather than seeking solutions in quick fixes, is the answer. If you really think about it, engaging difficult realties is, by definition, the job of the executive.

You should always be suspicious of the snake-oil salesman, regardless of how he or she may appear to you. Whether it's the employee who promises to fix everything, the consultant who has the perfectly packaged solution, or the computer system that claims to answer all your needs—whatever the guise, magical solutions, in reality, *do not exist.* The only path to success is to follow the natural, unavoidable laws of nature. There are no shortcuts.

Step 3: Take positive action in the direction of your fear.

Write down all of the ongoing problems in your current job. Next to each problem, list the major actions you are taking in response to it. Now, carefully examine each action and ask yourself whether this is helping to solve the problem or to avoid it? Is this a solution or a cover-up?

NOTES

1. John Micklethwait and Adrian Wooldridge, *The Witch Doctors: Making Sense of the Management Gurus* (New York: Times Business, 1996).
2. Frank Baum, *The Wonderful World of Oz* (New York: G. M. Hill Co., 1900).
3. Ibid.

SEVEN

Fear of the Unknown: What Is Lurking Out There?

No Exit

Sometimes, what you don't know seems more frightful than the pain you do know. That's exactly what Jean-Paul Sartre's play *No Exit* is all about. It opens with a hotel room in Hell, sparely furnished in Second Empire style and with an image of Eros on the mantel. Into this chilling room the bellhop introduces three permanent guests, one by one.

The first, Garcin, is a middle-aged pacifist journalist, who has just been shot as an army deserter. Bearing the heavy guilt of having deserted his comrades, what he now most seeks is to be told that his attempt to escape to Mexico and publish a pacifist magazine was heroic; he wants to hear that he was not a coward. The second guest, Inez, is an angry woman who lost her life when her roommate turned on the gas secretly in her apartment, killing her while she slept. She immediately despises the sniveling Garcin, who is to be her companion here forever, and she gives him no comfort whatsoever in his need. Nor will he receive any comfort from the next and final guest, Estelle, a promiscuous young woman who had drowned her illegitimate child and driven her lover to suicide.

Estelle, of course, becomes immediately interested in Garcin, whose craving for absolution obliterates any passion he might conjure up for the woman. Inez blocks every attempt they make to reach some kind of accord, while trying to befriend Estelle, who has no interest in friendship with the frightfully cold and angry Inez.

When these three guests—so tortuously matched—have brought their unrelenting demands on each other to a fevered pitch of frustration, escape becomes the only possible relief to their suffering. Just then, the locked door of their room swings open, showing outside an azure void. The guests, stunned by this sudden change of events, stare into the empty space. Nobody leaves. The door swings shut, and they are locked forever in their chosen cell.

Sartre's depiction of the feared unknown is haunting. Despite the suffering of the guests, they prefer their pain to exploring the unknown of the azure void. In their minds, the devil they know is better than the devil they don't know.

The fear of the unknown has been the bane of the businessperson for centuries. What if the new product doesn't sell as well as previous products? What if the competition introduces something better and cheaper? What if costs rise? If we allow it to happen, the unknown answers to all these questions can strike fear in our hearts and influence our decisions.

DISNEY

Walt Disney, the undisputed master of twentieth-century animated entertainment, spent most of his life battling with others who were fearful of change. His success, now legendary, wasn't so obvious during much of his life. He challenged every institution of the entertainment industry with his radical ideas, from the banks that financed motion pictures to the studios that produced them. He pulled that industry, kicking and screaming, into what would become the extraordinarily profitable field of color, talking, full-length, animated, feature films. In addition, he virtually created the field of cross-marketing merchandise with films.

The story of Walt Disney's incredible talent and success begins with his childhood. Walt's father, Elias Disney, had an extraordinary temper, and he often beat Walt and his brother Roy. To escape those childhood pains, Walt created stories of imaginary friends, which he eventually drew in cartoon form on paper. Throughout his teenage years, including his stint as an ambulance driver for the Red Cross during World War I while he was only sixteen, he continued to draw cartoons for his own amusement and that of his fellows.

After the war, Walt returned home and took a job as a graphic artist for the Kansas City advertising firm of Pesmen-Rubin. It was there that the eighteen-year-old Walt became interested in the new medium of animated films. Shortly thereafter, he signed on as an illustrator (for forty dollars a week) with the Kansas City Film Ad Company, which made sixty-second animated cartoon advertisements that appeared in movie theaters prior to the feature film.

After two years of creating animated advertising, Walt decided that animated films were not just suited for advertising—they could actually be entertaining as full-length feature films. He left Kansas City for California, only to discover that the Hollywood establishment was unwilling to consider his "radical" ideas about animated films. Animation was a fine technique for short advertisements, but nothing more.

Unable to land a job at a studio, Walt decided to start his own studio in the garage of his uncle Robert, who also lived in Los Angeles. With his brother Roy, Walt opened the Disney Brothers Studio. After a few years of struggle, Disney Brothers finally realized Walt's dream with the success of the film *Plane Crazy*, which starred a manic little mouse by the name of Mickey. *Plane Crazy* was a small but instant success. Disney quickly followed it with another film starring Mickey Mouse, titled *The Gallopin' Gaucho.*

Still unable to convince major distributors that animated films would attract audiences, Disney was plagued with distribution problems. Although few theaters carried the films, audiences thrilled at the sight of moving cartoons.

After the October 1927 premiere of the *Jazz Singer,* the first film to synchronize sound with action, Disney decided to produce a film in which Mickey talked. In *Steamboat Willie,* the third Mickey Mouse film, Walt combined the art of animation with voice-overs (he used his own falsetto voice for Mickey). The film was a roaring success, and it changed the struggling studio's fortunes forever.

By this time, other major studios were taking notice, and Universal offered to buy out Disney Brothers. Still convinced that his animated films would be a veritable gold mine, Walt refused to sell. In time, Disney Brothers became the most successful of all the motion picture studios.

The fear of the unknown kept the major studios from venturing into the animated film market that Disney ultimately created. At that time, as now, the major studios had rigid formulas for what they thought the public wanted to see on film, and Disney's unproved idea didn't fit into their formula. The major studios' fear of the unknown created the space for Disney to prosper. What the studios lost through fear, Disney quite successfully captured.

PRISONERS OF THE KNOWN

Stories of executives and organizations limited by the fear of the unknown abound. The high-tech giant Hewlett-Packard (HP) rejected the idea of manufacturing and selling personal computers during the late 1970s. What did the average person need with a computer? Why would they buy it?

The same thing had happened earlier with Swiss watchmakers. In 1967, the Swiss watch manufacturers invented electronic quartz movement watches at their research institute in Neufchatel, yet they rejected the idea of manufacturing such a watch. Who would want a watch without a spring? In the next decade, that decision caused the Swiss market share of the watch market to drop from 65 percent to less than 10 percent, as the Japanese capitalized on the electronic watch the Swiss had invented but refused to make.

UNAVOIDABLE CHANGE

As with other fears, the fear of the unknown causes you to avoid change. You know what is happening now, but since the future is unknown you cling tightly to the present. Even when the present is painful, the unknown future is frightening and you choose to stay in your pain.

The avoidance of change creates a difficult dilemma for you. Since everything is in constant change, clinging to the present takes a great deal of energy. Not only must you sabotage the natural course of oncoming change but you have to work endlessly at maintaining the illusion of sameness.

Change has always been the essence of life and always will be. I once heard that the last thing Adam told Eve before leaving the Garden of Eden was: "I believe we're living in an age of transition." Sound familiar?

The fear of the unknown blinds you to the possibilities of the future. You become frozen in the status quo, a prisoner of the known rather than inventors of the future. As executives, when you succumb to this fear, you create your own obsolescence in a business world that demands you continually change in order to embrace the future.

BREAKING THE CYCLE OF FEAR

Step 1: Acknowledge and confront the irrational beliefs that underlie your fear of the unknown.

Irrational Belief #1: What worked in the past will work in the future.

If anything has been proven to be true in recent business history, it is that what worked yesterday may not work tomorrow. The much-lamented truth that "change is here to stay" is a fact in business. Past success is no predictor of future success.

Every industry has experienced this, but perhaps none so blatant as the publishing industry. The phenomenal successes of *Reengineering the Corporation* and *The Pursuit of Excellence* were not repeated by the hundreds of books that followed using similar formulas. The best-selling nonfiction book of 1997, *Don't Sweat the Small Stuff,* was little more than a compilation of other relatively unknown self-help books. The fact that those books didn't necessarily sell well, while *Don't Sweat the Small Stuff* sold millions, completely baffled the publishing world. The kind of book that sells well today might do poorly tomorrow, and vice versa.

The hard lesson that executives in the publishing industry and in all other businesses have had to learn is that there is no substitute for keeping one's ear to the ground and taking an intelligent risk. The executive who wants to succeed in this environment has no choice but to trust her talents.

Intelligent risk is the antidote to the fear of the unknown. Knowing that anything is *possible,* you realize that some things are more *probable.* Based on your best ability, you anticipate what is probable and make decisions on that assessment. The question is not "Will change happen?" but rather "Where will change take me?"

> I am convinced that the only way to get ahead in this world is to live and sell dangerously.[1]
>
> John H. Johnson, Founder & CEO,
> Johnson Publishing Company
> (International publisher of *Ebony* magazine)

Confidence in your own abilities tells us that there is no boogeyman hiding under the darkness of the unknown. You are perfectly equipped to handle whatever situation the future brings. There is no reason for you to fear the future.

Irrational Belief #2: Don't move forward until you can predict success.

What makes you a successful executive is not the ability to completely predict the future, but confidence in your talents. A great example of this comes from HP's former chief executive, Lew Platt. Mr. Platt told a *Business Week* reporter in 1997 that HP "will fundamentally change the way people think about photography."

Photography? HP? At the time he made the statement, HP had little experience in manufacturing cameras or any other photographic equipment, much less in selling it. Perhaps Eastman Kodak, Canon, or Nikon would say this, but not HP. Mr. Platt was simply affirming his confidence in the talent at HP—talent that has proven to be very valuable, again and again. Why shouldn't it make a difference in the new world of digital photography?

This isn't the first time that HP has faced the unknown with steady confidence. Back in the early 1980s, HP had a vision of taking two printer technologies, laser and inkjet, and selling them to every personal computer owner. At the time, dot matrix printing was the noisy, cumbersome standard while inkjet and laser printing were relatively new technologies. Companies like Okidata and NCR owned the market for dot matrix printers, not HP. Nevertheless, HP executives stood confident in their talent to overtake the computer printer market.

As you probably know, HP did more than just become a player in the printer market. Today, HP owns 50 percent of the inkjet printer market and a whopping 60 percent of the laser printing market. Seventy percent of all computers sold today are bundled with an HP printer.

Will HP become a dominant player in the unknown future of digital photography? No one knows yet. One thing is certain, however. The talent of HP will have a defining impact on the technology of digital photography.

When you shrink back in fear from the unknowable future, you put yourself at a startling disadvantage. Whether you will reach your goals or not is not known, but when you approach the future with confidence in your talents you will come out ahead, whatever the final result.

Down through history the lesson has always been the same: It isn't our lack of ability that prevents us from successfully navigating change, it is our fear. When you plant your feet firmly in the ground, fearful of the oncoming march of time, you invite failure.

Irrational Belief #3: Someone else can accurately predict the future.

Executives sometimes believe that the unknown can be controlled by finding the right expert with a crystal ball. They believe that the right person can actually predict the future for them and relieve their fear of the unknown.

The truth is that no one can predict the future accurately. No one. Some have an educated hunch, but no one has a magical crystal ball. The industry of gurus, mystics, and futurists that purport to tell us what the future holds is enjoying a very profitable rise. Many of the more famous psychics now list on their résumés the corporate CEOs who are their regular clients. Oh, if it were only true! Wouldn't it be great to find that one person with a supernatural connection to the future?

The reality is that no one can accurately see the future. Executives who are successful take their best guess and *create the future*. Rather than wasting your time on finding someone who will read the corporate tea leaves, research the trends and then take action. By investing your energies in making something happen rather than simply reacting to a prediction, you greatly increase your chances of future success.

Step 2: Make a conscious effort to push past the fear even though you continue to feel it.

Every executive, no matter how experienced or successful, is uneasy whenever he or she sails into uncharted waters. Frankly, it's a feeling of vulnerability: a feeling that something unexpected might happen.

The real challenge is to learn that the unexpected can happen at any time, and to make peace with that. Even when you desperately cling to the status quo, you are no less vulnerable to the whims of unexpected circumstances. None of us completely controls our environment and all of us are vulnerable in some way. Moving into unknown territory isn't necessarily more risky than staying put, and it may actually be safer.

The issue at hand is how much you trust your talents to lead you. How equipped are you to handle all the curveballs your environment throws at you? If you are not able to handle these unexpected events very well, perhaps you're in the wrong environment? When you truly find the right match between your talents and your job—and that match *does* exist—you find that you are also equipped to handle the unexpected. You may never be completely comfortable with the surprise element, but you can reach a point where you no longer fear it. This is where you must put yourself to become a successful executive.

If you find that you are having a difficult time with the unknown, ask yourself whether it is because you're in a situation that doesn't match your talents. Perhaps your fear of the unknown is only a symptom of being in over your head. If this is your situation, consider carefully whether you are in the right job, company, or industry. You've got what it takes to succeed; you only need to find where your talents are needed.

Step 3: Take positive action in the direction of your fear.

One effective method of engaging the future without trying to perfectly predict it is that of scenario planning. Arie de Geus, in his book *The Living Company,* describes the scenario planning method in which Royal Dutch/Shell anticipated the future during his tenure as a senior executive at that company. In 1968, Shell began to use a method called "scenario planning," in which likely future scenarios are explored in depth.

According to de Geus:

> The scenario planners tried to grasp what was chang-
> ing in a wide variety of arenas: social values, technol-
> ogy, consumption patterns, political thinking, and
> international finance in the world at large. There was
> little duplication with the planning still done by
> Shell supply or finance people, who were looking
> only at oil-related developments. The new planners
> did not ignore oil and energy concerns, but they
> were looking for "driving forces," which might come
> from anywhere and ultimately work through to af-
> fect the world of energy and oil. They analyzed these
> forces to see whether, and how, the resulting changes
> might affect their own businesses. In short, scenarios
> provide tools through which the nonfashionable
> and weak signals may be picked up and considered,
> without overwhelming the managers who use them.
>
>   The various scenarios, which are explored and
> distilled, are then distributed to managers in an eas-
> ily readable format. The result? Scenarios force the
> management team to consider the future in real
> terms. "The scenario gives them a context for consid-
> ering all of these forces—perhaps not comprehen-
> sively, in the manner of an academic dissertation,
> but dynamically. A story of a falling oil price can
> bring all of these forces vividly to life in the imagina-

tion, so that they linger in 'memories of the future,' in words that are understandable to colleagues."[2]

The value of this type of planning isn't necessarily in the accuracy of the forecast. Rather, its real value is in the *engagement of the future*. These scenarios force you to embrace the future and all the possibilities. No matter which scenario actually manifests itself, you will have shed the fear that could have paralyzed you in the face of an uncertain future.

Consider a current project on which you are working. Draw a diagram to map out all the various scenarios that might develop. Now, from where you are today, what course of action seems to fit the most likely scenario?

There is no reason for us to construct a wall between the future and ourselves, yet we sometimes do so eagerly. Our real enemy isn't the future; it is the wall. It isn't a safe refuge that we create, but a trap that holds us back and ultimately starves us. It is our hesitation to enter the unknown that is our true enemy.

NOTES

1. John Johnson, *Succeeding against the Odds* (Amistad Press, 1989).
2. Aire de Geus, *The Living Company* (Cambridge, Mass.: Harvard Business School Press, 1997).

EIGHT

Fear of Authority: What If I Break the Rules?

THE FARM

In 1945, the British author George Orwell published a brilliant satire on the nature of totalitarianism entitled *Animal Farm*. The story is simple and poignant.

One night when Farmer Jones has gone to bed drunk, all the animals of Manor Farm assemble in the barn for a meeting. Old Major, the prize pig, wants to tell them about a strange dream he had. First, he tells them in clear, powerful language about "the nature of life" as he has come to understand it. Animals toil, suffer, get barely enough to eat; as soon as they are no longer useful, they are slaughtered. And why? Because animals are enslaved by Man, "the only creature that consumes without producing." According to Old Major, there is only one solution: Man must be removed from the farm.

After a brief interruption Major sums his vision up: All animals are friends, and Man is their only enemy. Animals must avoid Man's habits: no houses, beds, clothes, alcohol, money, trade. Above all, "We are brothers. No animal must ever kill any other animal. All animals are equal." His dream is "of the earth as it will be when Man has vanished." Then he teaches them an old animal song, "Beasts of England," which the animals in his dream sang. The repeated singing of this revolutionary song throws the animals into a frenzy.

Old Major dies soon after, but the animals feel they should prepare for the Rebellion he preached. The work of teaching and organizing the others falls on the pigs, thought to be the cleverest animals. Snowball and Napoleon are "pre-eminent among the pigs"; and then there is Squealer, "a brilliant talker."

Mr. Jones drinks and neglects his farm more and more. One evening, when he has forgotten to feed them for more than a day, the animals break into the feed storehouse and begin helping themselves. Jones and his farmhands charge in, lashing with their whips. This is more than the hungry animals can bear and they fight back fiercely. The surprised and frightened men are driven from the farm. Unexpectedly, the Rebellion has been accomplished, and Jones is expelled. Now, Manor Farm, renamed Animal Farm, belongs to the animals.

No longer oppressed by Man, the animals decide to establish some ground rules for their newfound freedom, so they establish the seven commandments of animalism:

1. Whatever goes upon two legs is an enemy.
2. Whatever goes upon four legs, or has wings, is a friend.
3. No animal shall wear clothes.
4. No animal shall sleep in a bed.
5. No animal shall drink alcohol.
6. No animal shall kill any other animal.

And the seventh was the most important commandment of all:

7. All Animals Are Equal.

But in a matter of time numerous calamities threaten the survival of Animal Farm. The pigs, especially Napoleon, assume considerable power in the name of protecting the livelihood of the farm. Before long, the pigs begin walking on their hind legs, move into the farmhouse, and begin oppressing the animals, in much the same way as Farmer Jones had done years earlier.

Toward the end, Napoleon and the other pigs reduce the seven commandments to one, which is:

All Animals Are Equal, But Some Animals
Are More Equal Than Others.

It is a powerful story about commonly held beliefs of authority. As in *Animal Farm, many* people fear that no matter how well-intentioned, all authority is ruthless and ultimately self-serving. Although the story is most often interpreted as a clever satire on Marxist communism, Orwell insisted that it was a story about the fear of authority in modern society.

Animal Farm highlights an important difference between respect for authority and the fear of authority. The former is healthy, while the latter is ultimately destructive. A healthy respect for authority is one that views authority figures as necessary "organizing principals" in a group ("group" meaning anything from entire nations to small groups of people organized for a purpose). In other words, you respect persons in authority because they help an organization to stay focused and organized. Someone has to make the decisions, or in the words of one American President: The "buck" has to stop somewhere. Groups of people can't be held responsible for results as easily as an individual. Therefore, authority figures in an organization not only keep the organization focused, they bear the responsibility for its actions.

Very few of us would consciously disagree with the above characterization of authority. But many of us actually go further in our reaction to authority. We actually *fear* it. We imagine that authority figures have the power to diminish us, and what's worse, we believe they will do so if it serves their self-interest.

This fear of authority can have far-reaching effects on the success of an executive's career and it can manifest in any number of ways. Some executives develop a love/hate relationship with their superiors, whom they both obey and resent. Some solve this dilemma by setting their sights on becoming powerful, too, as a form of self-preservation. Other executives dominate their employees, fearful that an underling may challenge their authority and usurp their position. Even many senior executives hold these dark beliefs, fearful of their powerful colleagues, never trusting them, and always protecting their own turf.

This fear of authority has many faces in the modern business world. As with the other fears, it always has a detrimental effect on the organization and its executives. Following are just a few of the erroneous beliefs behind the fear.

AUTHORITY IS ALWAYS SELF-SERVING

In this view, those in authority have but one interest at heart: their own. The only reason they sought a position of power was to use other people to accomplish their own agenda. A position of authority gives them the right and privilege to press others into the service of their personal ambitions.

On the surface it may seem that anyone holding this belief would never last in a corporation, but this is absolutely not the case. In fact, many of those tormented by this fear of authority decide to "play along" with the game in order to become powerful themselves. Once they achieve a position of authority, then they too have earned the right to use others to fulfill their own agenda.

When you hold this belief, it leads to a deep resentment and suspicion of your superiors. You believe that, given the chance, your boss will do whatever is necessary to advance herself. You can never completely trust her or take what she tells you at face value. You must always be looking for the "real" motive behind her actions.

This fear of authority is the number one enemy of productive teams. Why should I be a team player, since the game is really "every man for himself?" I'll go along with you to a point, but I'm not willing to give 100 percent unless I am absolutely sure that I will benefit from my actions.

Executives who hold this belief are truly baffled by all the talk about teams and empowerment. After all, they put up with the self-serving wiles of their bosses, and they insist that their employees should do the same.

AUTHORITY IS ALWAYS RIGHT

The flip side of the fear of authority is the belief that those in authority are always right. Somehow, someway, they always know what is the right thing to do. Thus, authority figures must never be questioned and always obeyed. This belief leads you to usurp your own judgment and, instead, look to your superiors to make all the decisions. THEY know what is the right thing to do. THEY have the answers. THEY should tell me what to do.

So when your boss makes a mistake (as he inevitably will), it triggers enormous anger. When it becomes apparent that he didn't know it all, you withdraw your respect and loyalty. You cannot follow a leader who is merely human.

THE ONLY PATH TO SUCCESS IS TO APPEASE AUTHORITY

The fear of authority can make you the quintessential brown-noser: "Authority figures control my success; therefore, the way to succeed is to please them. I must find out what they want from me, and then do whatever that is. Rather than focusing on how to do my job best, I must find out how my boss wants me to do the job, and do that. Pleasing my superiors is my primary objective." As a result, you become unwilling to challenge the status quo. You are unwilling to explore new and better ways of doing your job; instead, you obsess on doing the job in a way that will win the boss' praise.

The fear of authority is the rigid backbone of the bureaucratic, hierarchical organization. It forms a long column of "back scratchers," each trying to please the one above him in order to achieve a semblance of success. In the process, the actual work of serving customers and increasing shareholder value takes a backseat to the organization pleasing itself.

BREAKING THE CYCLE OF FEAR

Step 1: Acknowledge and confront the irrational beliefs that underlie your fear of authority.

Irrational Belief #1: Powerful others determine my success.

One basis of the fear of authority is giving too much power to authority figures. In other words, you feel that you cannot succeed unless you first please those who are in authority. When you do this, you endow powerful others with more power than they really have.

Powerful people in your life can make certain tasks easier

for you, but rarely can they affect the totality of your career. A powerful politician may be able to get you into the finest school, but he can't make the grade for you. Likewise, a powerful boss may be able to give you a promotion, but she can't ensure that you do the job well.

When you imagine that authority figures have total power over you, you have given yourself over to fear. For if they can make you successful, then they can also make you fail. If they can help you, then they can also destroy you. When you believe this, you actually give them the power to run your life.

No one can control you unless you allow him or her to do so. No one can make your career or destroy your career without your participation. You *always* have a choice. Sometimes that choice isn't what you wish it could be, but you can always choose your behavior.

In many ways, by conferring the power of success or failure on authority figures, you are absolving yourself of responsibility. It's easier to blame the boss than it is to accept responsibility for your own behavior. It's easier to play the role of helpless victim than it is to try and solve a difficult situation.

Irrational Belief #2: Authority is always self-serving.

The darker side of the fear of authority is the belief that powerful others always act in their own self-interest. In this belief, you are only a pawn on the chessboard of life. While it is true that absolute power can corrupt, there are precious few people who ever attain absolute power. Everyone, no matter how powerful, answers to someone else. Only in the rare and isolated cases of total dictatorship is there absolute power—and even in those cases there is usually a constituency of people whom the dictator must please.

Absolute power is extremely rare in the corporation. Even those who might seem to have total control answer to boards of directors, shareholders, institutional investors, or powerful Wall Street analysts. Regardless of how it may seem on the surface, their decisions are rarely made independently.

Most authority figures in the corporation are more empathetic to those in their charge than you may think. Why?

Because anyone who has worked in an organization for a few years knows that someone at the bottom of the hierarchy can quickly move to the top. If you want your people to help you accomplish your goals, you need to have some sense of empathy for their situation. If you don't, chances are that you won't last long. No one wants to work with a tyrant.

When an executive complains about other senior executives who "have it out for me," it is usually the fear of authority speaking, not reality. Rather than deal with unpleasant or difficult realities, this executive has chosen to escape responsibility by blaming his superiors. A boss can place some restrictions on you, but only a fool would prevent you from achieving success. After all, in most organizations a boss' success is determined primarily by the success of her employees.

Ultimately, no one can change your talents. Even when there is an abuse of power, you must remain confident of the fact that there is nothing that person can do to harm your essential being. Who you are and what you are capable of accomplishing is firmly planted within you and is always under your control. Should an authority figure try to block that expression of yourself, it must be seen for what it is—an *abuse* of authority. It is not power that corrupts—it is the false belief in your own *powerlessness*.

Step 2: Make a conscious effort to push past the fear even though you continue to feel it.

The roots of these fearful feelings about authority very often extend back into your childhood. Through your parents or other significant authority figures, you learn to fear those who are in positions of power. Here's the catch: You fear them, but you also need them. It is a difficult bind that remains with you into adulthood.

Step 3: Take positive action in the direction of your fear.

Which authority figures in your life elicit love/hate feelings from you? You need them, but you resent them for their perceived control. Make a conscious effort to see these authority figures not as surrogate parents, but as human beings like yourself.

Start by making a list of all the strengths and weaknesses of those in positions of authority over you. Carefully examine your list. The next time you encounter each one of these people, review the list in your mind. Think about this person's struggles and triumphs. The more of a human face you put upon the authority figure, the less you will fear it.

NINE

Fear of Aging:
What If I'm Obsolete?

Becoming obsolete is a choice, not a product of aging. Growing older is an excuse some people choose to remove themselves from the fast lane of business, and while slowing down is a choice we may all make at different points in our lives, it isn't the inevitable result of growing older.

One of my dearest friends, Ruth, is a woman who has had several fascinating and very successful careers. Along the way, she has been a health-care worker, president of the league of women voters, and a consultant with the United Nations. Ruth is now solidly in her seventies, and she keeps a pace that would seem to exhaust most of us but only invigorates her more. I have never met anyone more capable of learning and with more stamina than Ruth. Last we spoke, she was rushing to finish a white paper for a staff member at the White House on the mental health conditions in Kosovo (where she worked during the military action there) before leaving to spend three months in Somalia, where she will work with the local officials to create self-sustaining farming operations. After that, it is on to Israel to participate in a conference on the elusive peace in the Middle East.

And Ruth is no exception. My own father is a computer whiz at the young age of 73. A civil engineer who spent most of his life leaning over a drafting table, he learned the art of computer-aided drafting (CAD) in his sixties. He became such an expert that the local college recruited him to teach their new graduates CAD. His only complaint with teaching was that his students (mostly recent high school graduates) lacked the focus and motivation to learn the sometimes tedious computer skills necessary!

THE GRAY-HAIRED EXECUTIVE

Several year ago I wrote a book about downsizing. As I traveled the country, I often encountered executives (mostly men) in their fifties and sixties complaining that the corporate world no longer had a place for them. Indeed, much of my own research had uncovered that large numbers of older (but hardly retirement age) workers were becoming unemployed through layoffs. It seemed to me to be a paradox; after all, most senior executives across this country sport a fair amount of gray hair (if they have any hair left). So why would they be discriminating against their peers?

What I have come to discover is that the problem is much more complex. Most companies that I work with are truly eager to hire experienced (read: *older*) workers. The problem, however, was expressed to me this way by a senior vice president of one of America's largest corporations:

> I jump at the chance to hire older workers, I really do. But a fair number of the older workers I interview make it very hard to hire themselves. It's almost as if they come into the interview with a list of all the things they won't do. Sort of like the housekeeper who starts out saying she doesn't do windows or laundry. Hell, there's nothing around here that I won't do myself if I need to! Why should I hire someone my own age who is sending off all kinds of signals about what they won't do at the start?

This same senior executive told me that motivated older workers are often the best hires he makes, and he recalled a number of specific examples. They bring experience and stability—two important assets that most younger workers don't have. They've already been through the school of hard knocks and earned some pretty impressive degrees there. If they've survived that many years in a profession, they had to learn a little something along the way.

Deloitte & Touche, one of America's largest consulting firms, used to focus only on hiring new graduates, but today it is hiring from all age brackets. Jim Wall, who is in charge of hiring at Deloitte & Touche, says of the trend toward hiring older and more seasoned consultants: "We need people with practice and experience."[1]

Over and over again I find the same story to be true. Companies are eager to hire and promote older workers. So why are so many of them "early retired"? One early retiree explained it to me like this: "I don't want to prove myself to a company again." In other words, he didn't want to work that hard to move up the ladder—he wanted credit for what he had done at another company during another time. So instead of buckling down to a new job, he opted to retire with a little less than full retirement and to exit the working world.

It may be bemoaned, but this is a fact about working today: No matter how old you are, how prestigious your degree is, or how well-connected you are, you've got to produce to stay employed. The days of simply showing up at the office to collect a paycheck are over. This is especially hard for some people to accept because they watched some other workers before them slack off as they grew older. One older executive said it best: "It used to be a rite of passage to slow down the older you got. People thought it was respectful to let you be mediocre."

The easy answer here is to say that the business world is prejudiced against older workers, but most of the evidence is to the contrary. Even Dilbert lampoons the fact that gray hair is "executive hair." Our culture still pays heavy respect to the wisdom and authority of older people. Think about it. If you were going to invest most of your life savings in only one company, would you feel more comfortable with a company run by a twenty-something CEO or one run by a fifty- or sixty-something? I think most of us would take the latter. The twenty-something might quickly make a great deal of money or, with the same speed, lose all of our money, but we'd trust the fifty-something to be more careful with our investment.

So the point is this: There is no justification for the fear of aging. The vast majority of us will stay healthy, alert, and active until long after we've reached an acceptable retirement age. The older you get, the more practice you have at being great. If you want to work and are willing to accept a paycheck that matches your performance and not your age, you can.

The hard truth is that the fear of aging is something that starts within us and that we project on to the people around us. Because we worry that we are somehow diminished with age (or will be diminished with age), we begin to create that reality around us. Like with all the fears we have discussed, the more you fear something, the more energy you put into creating what you fear.

Beyond simply worrying about employment as we age, the fear of aging can have a far more intrusive effect on our career. Because this fear is so intimately personal, it strikes at the core of what we believe to be true about ourselves and the meaning of life. When those issues aren't resolved, the fear of aging can seep into our careers and ultimately destroy them. Two ways this can happen are mania and excessive control.

IF YOU LOOK BUSY, YOU CAN'T BE OBSOLETE

Busy, busy, busy. Can't sit still. Don't want to be alone. Must be on the go all of the time. She leaves for work early, checking her office voice mail on her cellular phone on the way to work. Her day is scheduled tightly with meetings she has called concerning any number of matters. She meets with employees over lunch and returns to her office quickly to check her voice mail and e-mail. There are afternoon meetings, and then reports and letters to write. At the end of the day, she leaves late, runs to her exercise class, and then to a late supper. Exhausted, she falls into bed, only to wake early the next day to repeat the whole cycle.

This executive's life is on the fast track, moving so swiftly there isn't time for anxieties about life to bubble up through the mania. By running constantly, she is trying to escape the fear of obsolescence through hyperactivity. Her busy life isn't fulfilling, but it is overflowing with activity. With her frantic motions she is saying "I am here; I am competent."

Of course, it is important to say that not every busy executive is trying to prove his or her competence. I am speaking of the executives who intentionally fill their working hours with activity for the sake of busyness. They call meetings frequently, filling their time with activity that isn't always necessary to the job. They extend the scope of their jobs, inadvertently taking on the tasks of other executives. While privately complaining about their hectic schedules, the reality is that the mania helps them to bury their fear.

A recent phenomenon closely related to the fear of obsolescence is what the pundits have labeled "stress envy." Stress envy is the feeling that if you *aren't stressed*, you must not be important. After all, important people are constantly being paged, faxed, and called and are always in a meeting. If you aren't, what's wrong with you?

OUT OF CONTROL

If we dig a little deeper into the fear of obsolescence we find that it originates in the more sinister fear of death. The fear of death isn't exactly common conversation among executives, but it can be very much a part of the background.

An executive can control many things, but death is not one of them. We may try to prolong our life and do what we can to avoid disease and injury, but ultimately we cannot control death. In time it comes, and in its grip, we are all defenseless.

Until we no longer feel a need to control death, we are compelled to control life. Everything, every situation, everyone in our life must submit to our will. By arranging our life and environment, we can briefly fool ourselves into feeling that nothing can affect us without our permission.

When the executive who fears obsolescence finds herself in a situation in which she isn't in control, she feels terribly anxious, and she must take control or she leaves. When she is out of control, she feels vulnerable to her repressed fears that something may overtake her at any time. The unexpected and unstructured is highly threatening.

IT'S NEVER TOO LATE TO START

The fear of being obsolete can convince you that you are too old to start a new business or to try another career track. You tell yourself that at your age you'd be better off sticking with what you know rather than chasing some dream.

Imagine the risk Ronald Reagan took in 1966 when he left a long career as a successful actor and corporate spokesperson to run for governor of California. Not only had he never held public office, it was only two years earlier that he had joined the Republican party. At that time he was fifty-five years old. Then, he did it again in 1978 at the age of 67 when he decided to run for President after failing twice before. While he had some experience in politics at that point, he certainly had no experience in national politics and was a complete novice at the political wrangling within the Washington beltway, a skill that is so essential to success.

As was true for Reagan, a fresh start is possible at any age, if you so choose. There is no reason success cannot be yours at any age unless you limit yourself. You are only obsolete when you choose to stop learning and not before.

BREAKING THE CYCLE OF FEAR

Step 1: Acknowledge and confront the irrational beliefs that underlie your fear of aging.

Irrational Belief #1: My abilities diminish with age.

Some of the most talented, hardest working executives in the world are over seventy years old. They love what they do and only get better as the years go by. Everywhere you look, you see older executives achieving unprecedented success. Think about Alan Greenspan, chairman of the Federal Reserve; Robert Pew, chairman of Steelcase, Inc.; and David Murdock, CEO of Dole Foods, all of whom were in their seventies at the time they held these positions. The list of highly successful, older executives is long indeed. The only thing that limits these executives is their desire to postpone a comfortable retirement. As long as they want to work, they will be extremely competent.

If anything, the practice that comes with age enhances your talents. It takes a great deal to rattle the cage of someone who has had a long career. That kind of wisdom and experience is priceless. The bottom line is this: You're limited by your age only if you believe your age limits you.

Step 2: Make a conscious effort to push past the fear even though you continue to feel it.

The executive who is running from death is not headed toward a goal. She is fleeing the loss of herself. She cannot stop lest she becomes overcome with anxiety. Burning questions pursue her: "What is my life about?" "What is meaningful?" "What is my purpose?"

When you come to terms with the meaning of your life, you make peace with your aging and ultimately your demise. Your life becomes directed and focused rather than a loose collection of activities. What is important in life becomes clear, and you work toward that end. You may work hard and long, but you also understand the importance of quiet contemplation, of spontaneity, and of peace of mind. When you are fleeing the loss of self, you cannot afford these moments of respite, lest you become consumed with the feeling of fear.

Until you confront the meaning of life, you cannot reach your highest potential. The dark cloud of death hangs over you, preventing you from allowing the powerful river of life and talent to flow from you. Instead, you waste energy on hyperactivity, domination, and overcontrol.

The meaning of life is a deeply personal lesson that no one can teach. Rabbis, ministers, therapists, teachers, family, and friends can all help, but the ultimate answer comes from within. There is no substitute for the struggle to understand and accept one's purpose in life.

Step 3: Take positive action in the direction of your fear.

How have you limited yourself because you thought you were too old to learn something new? The truth is you may not *want* to learn something new, but you can if you choose. Your beliefs, not your age, limit you.

What is it that you have always wanted to do, but have given up? Remember how you wanted to sail around the world or write a novel? You're never too old to try, much less succeed. By giving yourself permission to try, you will set yourself free in all areas. All you need is to show yourself just how much you can accomplish.

NOTES

1. Leslie Kaufman, "Failed at Your Last Job? Wonderful! You're Hired," *New York Times*, October 6, 1999.

PART TWO
TALENT: YOUR STRONGEST SUIT

TEN

Talent Is the DNA of Your Destiny

HAPPINESS COMES FROM USING YOUR TALENTS, NOT FROM WHAT YOUR TALENTS ACHIEVE

There is a powerful force inside you. It is more than enough, more than what you will ever use. If you tap into this power—and you can—you will find yourself on a path that leads to your greatest potential. It is the path of all truly great executives.

Over the years I've had the pleasure of working with some of America's most successful executives. I've also had the opportunity to be in the presence of many others. And my experience—as most who work with these executives also experience—is that there is something intangibly great that I sense while in their presence. It is self-confidence, yet much more. It is determination, focus, execution, and more. There is an air of leadership that attracts to it everyone they encounter. Even when others don't like this executive, they are drawn to follow him or her. They *want* to make this executive successful.

This book is about the fearless power behind such executives. More importantly, it is about how you can tap into this very same force and use it to become your personal best. And that incredible force is found only in your talent. What's more, I believe that your talent is the expression of your *spiritual self*. Of course, I can't prove this, but I can direct you to compelling evidence all around you. Take a hard look at the people working around you. Notice the ones who are truly practicing their talents at work. What do you see? It's more than just a skilled person performing a task. They seem to create opportunities for success all around themselves. The right opportunities always seem to fall in their laps and their energy seems to be boundless. Whether or not you can join me in believing that this is something truly spiritual, you must admit that it is *powerful*. It's what we all want.

While we cannot see talent directly, we can see it at work in our lives. Each of us, whether or not we believe in our talents, allows talent to show every day. How? By doing well tasks that we take for granted. Doing these things seems so natural, like a no-brainer. With grace and ease we do them, sometimes completely unaware of the power we are calling into use. The use of our talents is so natural to our being that it is only through unnatural circumstances that we become alienated from our talent.

And this is the simple, but overwhelmingly profound secret of great executives: *They believe wholeheartedly and without reservation in their talents.* They know there is no situation that they cannot handle. No matter how tough the journey, their talents will lead them to their destiny.

That's not to say that these executives are always successful or even that they expect to have a perfect scorecard. What they believe—and you must too if you wish to be successful—is that whatever the final result, their talents have guided them to the best possible outcome. Even if that outcome appears to be a temporary "failure," they know that they have made the best decision at the time. They trust themselves. They trust their talent to lead them.

If you choose to trust your talent, you will be ready for whatever task you encounter. Right now, you have all the talent you will ever need. Everything necessary to reach your personal best is inside you at this moment. Your ultimate business success is within your reach. You have been given wonderful and immensely powerful tools to accomplish your highest mission in work and in life. Your talents are gifts, and they are the seeds of your destiny. Your business success depends solely on what you do with these unique gifts.

This simple, but elusive truth has been born out through the ages, since commerce began. People of all walks of life—rich, poor, smart, uneducated, able-bodied, disabled, articulate, bashful—have all succeeded in business. Successful executives come in as many different packages as there are people. The one common element—the only common element—that links all successful executives is this: They discover their unique blend of talents and trust it completely. Executive success is really just that simple.

It is tragic that so many misguided leadership "experts" have for decades told us how to become successful executives. What to say, how to act, what to wear, where to educate ourselves, how to climb the career ladder—the list of advice goes on and on. None of it has a solid basis in reality or research.

Behavioral scientists, too, have tried for years to predict who will become a successful executive and who will not (most notably William Byham's twenty-year experiment with assessment centers at AT&T). The result? None of the several hundred well-designed studies has been able to predict consistently the qualities of an emerging business leader. Not one. There is no test that will predict who will become a successful executive. There is no one list of leadership "qualities." Despite our best efforts, we are incapable of determining who will become a successful executive.

Why is this? Because business success comes only from the natural blossoming of our individual, idiosyncratic talents. When we allow ourselves to discover and develop that talent, we grow into the path of leadership that is meant for us. That path may be dramatically different from all other paths, but it is right and successful for us. This is the only path to leadership. It is the only path to achieving our best.

And despite our most treasured fantasies of becoming something different, more, smarter, or supertalented, we cannot escape our innate abilities. What makes executives successful is a confident reliance on their particular strengths. So it is with you: What will make you successful is not imitating someone else's success, but realizing your own potential. Once you grasp this, you will be on your way to achieving your highest potential. Success lies not in acquiring something outside of yourself or being something else, but in *maximizing* the talent you already have.

You are a portfolio of talents. This portfolio (which is within you at this very moment) is all you will ever have. Your challenge lies in leveraging those talents maximally. You don't need to get something for success. You don't need to emulate someone else. All you need, you already own.

Think of your talent as the DNA of your destiny. Talent is the sacred seed of the life you are meant to have—the one you truly desire. It is your choice whether you will trust this seed and allow it to grow. You, and you alone, choose whether you will have complete fulfillment.

So forget the leadership books. Forget anything that tells you to be someone other than yourself. At best, it is wishful thinking that has little reliable evidence to support it. Empowerment, strategic planning, negotiating, resolving conflict, creating shared visions, and quality management—these are all great abilities that you will not find in each and every successful executive. Perhaps you will find one or two, and perhaps none. What you will find are a few talents that have been thoroughly developed and exploited.

TALENT IS THE GOLDEN KEY

One of the great myths about successful executives is that they are paid for their time. Nothing is further from the truth. Truly successful companies pay their executives for their talent, not their time. An executive who spends six hours at work fully employing her talent is worth far more than another who works twelve mediocre hours a day.

If you want to realize your highest potential, here's what you do: Decide what you do best, and do it often. Put yourself in situations where you can engage your finest ability. Acknowledge what you lack and do what is necessary to dilute the risk of your weaknesses, and—most importantly—spend your precious time and energy doing what you do best.

In my career as a management psychologist, I've spent years focusing on succession planning—the process of determining which executives will be promoted to high-level management positions. During that time, I've worked with thousands of executives in almost every industry imaginable. The one thread—the only thread—that connects all of those who have sustained successful, progressive careers is that they relied heavily upon their strengths. They didn't waste time in jobs that didn't tap their strongest talents. Nor did they waste time trying to do a job that they weren't capable of doing. Instead, they sought out environments where they could practice their talents and allow them to shine.

I have consistently found that those executives who focus on their talents are personally more fulfilled than those who don't. Even though their jobs are just as hectic, demanding, frustrating, challenging, and physically tiring as those of all the rest, they find themselves rejuvenated by doing their jobs. Instead of leaving work tired and mentally depleted, they leave tired but content at having engaged their talents. Their work has personal meaning and value.

Corporate life is full of temptation to abandon your personal talents. The next, better position may not be more meaningful, but it does offer a better salary, more corporate exposure, or a better title. And so does the next position. Within a few years, it is easy to find yourself in a job that has little meaning for you and that doesn't really tap your best abilities. It is the classic Peter Principle in operation: If we choose to allow it, we can be promoted into our highest level of incompetence.

So what restrains you? What holds you back from trusting and maximizing your talents? Fear. Fear tells you that you are inadequate for the challenges that face you each day. Fear tells you that you must be something more than what you are. Fear tells you that your gifts are not sufficient. Thus, fear steals from you the success that is your birthright. As an executive, your biggest career challenge is to conquer this fear, to see reality clearly, and to give your talents the space to grow and express their innate blessings. The fearless executive is the executive who completely trusts her talents.

THE CRUCIBLE OF TALENT

Talent is an intrinsic potential to do something well. It is the explosion of the human spirit into our everyday lives. At the point that you are reading this book, you already have your lifelong talents. What you do best is already determined, and should you choose to fully use your talents, you will realize this vast potential. What you become in life starts with talent and manifests itself in *what you do with that talent*. Any job—

anything—that prevents you from developing your unique talents diminishes both your ultimate fulfillment and achievement. It blocks you from being your best.

No one is without talent, and plenty of it. Everyone does some things better than others. Everyone has some glowing strengths that, if given the chance, can outshine their weaknesses.

Of course, this isn't to say that we can all be the very best at what we do. But it is to say that we can definitely be our *personal best*. We can achieve the highest level of success of which we are capable. We can be at our finest. We can have the life we truly desire.

To begin understanding what talent is, there are two other things you must get to know: *advantages* and *skills*. Because both of these things are often wrongly confused with talent, let's take a quick look at them.

ADVANTAGES

Advantages are things that give us an extra boost in life. They can be many things, but a few are a great education, wealth, high intelligence, and a charming personality. Advantages only *augment* talent—they can never substitute for it.

Sadly, corporate hiring practices often confuse advantages with talent. In fact, the writing of a résumé is inherently biased toward advantages because things like degrees, certificates, extracurricular activities, fellowships, and great references can be easily and succinctly written down. Talent, on the other hand, is very hard to describe in words, at least in a convincing manner. So many hiring managers often make the mistake of interpreting advantages as signs of talent when, in fact, they aren't. Some of the most well-written résumés filled with advantages come from aspiring executives who have yet to discover their real talent.

One of the best examples of how the advantage of education isn't a strong predictor of talent is the highly respected head of the Federal Reserve System, Alan Greenspan. Unless you were told, you might never guess that this financial genius received his degree from the Juilliard School of Music. Not exactly the place where you would expect to produce one of the leading financial minds of the country! The point to remember is that education can be a wonderful advantage, but it is not a reliable substitute for talent.

Advantages cannot replace your talent, but they can give it a great boost. If you have a talent for accounting, it helps a great deal to have a master's degree in accounting and to hold a CPA license. Or if you have a talent for managing high-tech businesses and processes, a Stanford MBA may help you enhance and refine those skills.

TALENT IS NOT INTELLIGENCE

As with education, high intelligence is not a talent but an advantage. Simply being "bright" doesn't guarantee that you can do whatever you choose to do well. In fact, high intelligence may simply mean that you did well on an IQ test!

In 1921, the famous Stanford University psychologist Louis Terman started a study of the impact of intelligence on lifelong outcomes. The study began with 1,470 genius-level children and followed them throughout their lifetimes. Since the life spans of these children exceeded the career of Terman, he transferred the study to Drs. Robert and Pauline Sears upon his retirement. After nearly a half century of study, the Sears published their results. What distinguished spectacular achievement from low achievement or failure among the study participants was "prudence and forethought, willpower, perseverance and desire. They chose among their talents and concentrated their efforts."[1] Those children, now well into their senior years, revealed that intelligence alone is not enough to guarantee success. Those who succeeded did so by persistently relying on their talent.

ACQUIRED SKILLS

The second thing often confused with talent is skills. Skills are learned abilities. They are something for which we do not necessarily have talent, but which we have learned to do by repetition. I'm sure each of us can list many skills we have learned, but which we don't particularly enjoy doing or for which we have little talent.

Talent Is Not Experience

One aspect of skills that is often confused with talent is working experience. Because someone has done a job for many years does not necessarily mean that he or she is good at the job or even capable of being good. For example, I might spend my entire career as an advertising copywriter, acquire all the knowledge of the field, and still not be very good at writing advertising copy.

Like education, talent thrives on experience. The person with a talent for a particular job generally grows in the job and develops with practice. As your experience increases, so does effectiveness. Experience refines and develops your talent. But experience at a job for which you have little talent produces consistently mediocre results, little personal growth, and worst of all prevents you from spending the same precious time and energy growing and succeeding in the area of your talents.

There is a well-known theory that "against the grain" job experiences challenge executives and cause them to develop new skills. As this plays out, junior executives are often moved through a series of disparate jobs, regardless of their interests, passions, or talents, under the guise of "developing" more well-rounded executives.

The truth is "against the grain" job experiences help an executive only to the extent that they impart new knowledge (i.e., familiarity with human resources regulations, accounting practices, regulatory standards), *but they do not develop new talent.* The executive that succeeds on such a career path is the one who finds opportunity in each job to practice his or her strengths. Challenging jobs do not create talent in the executive.

Now that we've explored what talent is and how it differs from advantages and skills, we're ready to dive in and discover our own talents. In the next chapter, we begin this process.

NOTE

1. Donald O. Clifton, *Soar with Your Strengths* (New York: Delacorte Press, 1992).

ELEVEN

Discovering Your Talent

"If only I had some talent." I hear this all the time from well-meaning people who have lost touch with themselves. "I can't do anything *special*," they tell me. I must disagree with this perception. Everyone has talent. Each person has certain strengths and interests that, although they may lie dormant, are contained within the self. There is overwhelming evidence to suggest that persons of every imaginable background, socioeconomic status, education, and personality profile have unique talents.

As we have seen, the primary block to your awareness of talent is fear. You limit yourself by fearing the outcome, to the point where you may not even allow those talents to surface in your awareness. Your fear inadvertently convinces you that you have no talent.

Fear is the master craftsman of censorship. Fear has prevented more businesses and careers from thriving and more art and literature from being born than have insufficient funds, lack of education, or censuring governments. So insidious is the work of fear that it not only prevents you from actualizing your talents, it can hide those talents from your conscious mind.

Once we work on eliminating the fear, the talent begins to emerge. We don't have to labor at "finding" our talent or go on an arduous quest for it; talent naturally fills the space vacated by fear. When we are free from the limits of fear, we can explore the world and respond in ways that are natural and satisfying. Without effort, we find ourselves practicing our talents.

The birthing of a talent is an uncontrollable, natural process. While we cannot force it, there are several common hallmarks of an emerging talent. Let's take a look at three of them.

YEARNINGS

The first hallmark of talent is a yearning. A yearning is a pull toward some activity and is most often felt after we watch someone else engaged in that activity. It is a heartfelt magnetism that tugs at us and urges us to action.

Bruce Hangen, conductor of the Omaha Symphony Orchestra, describes one of his earliest yearnings to be conductor: "Just sitting there in my position as first cellist, I knew I wanted to get up and lead the orchestra, and I knew I could do it better than my teacher."[1] Shortly thereafter, Hangen's junior high music teacher handed him the baton and his career as a conductor was launched.

Another prominent example of a yearning happened to a young Fred Smith. During his junior year at Yale, Smith wrote a paper that described a hub-and-spokes system of overnight freight forwarding. Smith was mesmerized by the possibilities of such an efficient system, which he imagined could be comprised of both airline and truck routes. Despite the high cost of creating such a national system, which had to be fully functional on the first day of operation, Smith persisted with the idea after graduation. Numerous experts and business analysts had pronounced his idea impractical (starting with his Yale professor, who gave the paper a grade of C on the basis of feasibility), but Smith continued to pursue the idea. He eventually raised $72 million in investment capital and started the company known as Federal Express.

On March 12, 1973, Federal Express opened for business, sending its airplanes from all over the country (the "spokes") to Memphis (the "hub") to deliver an underwhelming total of six packages. After losing millions of dollars over the next few years, Federal Express eventually became profitable and today is the world's premier overnight delivery service—all starting from the yearning of a college student.

However, yearnings alone aren't sufficient to indicate talent. Certainly, everyone has had the experience of wanting to do something for which they weren't suited: write the great

American novel, sing at the Metropolitan Opera, or cook a gourmet meal. These yearnings are generally fantasies that are based on desires for fame, glamour, or excitement.

A great example of misleading yearnings based on glamour is a study conducted by SRI Gallup on flight attendants for a major airline. What the study found was that flight attendants who were enticed into the profession by the perceived glamour of travel to exotic locations tended to have poor performance records and short-lived careers (eighteen months or less). Those who became flight attendants because they enjoyed making other people comfortable were generally highly rated and tended to have a long-term career with the airline.

Yearnings, while not sufficient to indicate talent, always surround talent. We are naturally drawn to do those things for which we have potential for excellence. Yearnings are one of nature's pointers to our highest good.

SATISFACTION

Another hallmark of talent is satisfaction. When we engage in activities for which we have talent, it feels good, especially when we notice that our skill is improving with practice. There is a strong feeling of contentment—that we are doing something that is meaningful—when we engage our talent.

Once, while working with a national retailer, I encountered two district managers who, with the exception of different territories, had identical jobs. Both had equally experienced store managers reporting to them and their sales numbers were roughly equivalent. One of the managers, Tom, had been a district manager for most of his career. Tom had worked for several national companies, and as is the case with most district managers, had spent much of his life traveling from one store to the next. Tom was in his early fifties and despite his age, kept up a grueling travel schedule. Tom was well-respected within the company and was often used as a mentor for new district managers.

Judy, the other district manager, had been in her position for more than a decade and was very ambitious. Unfortunately, Judy didn't have much talent for working with people, and her relationships with her store managers suffered badly as a result. I traveled with Judy for several days, visiting many of her stores with her. Each time we entered a store, I could see the dread on the faces of the store and department managers.

The differences between Tom and Judy were profound. No matter how hectic his schedule, Tom appeared rested and alert. He was attentive to the people around him and made them feel comfortable in his presence. Judy, on the other hand, always seemed stressed and a bit tired. She worked hard but didn't seem to enjoy her job.

Over several years, I worked with Judy as a consultant. In time, she admitted that she really disliked her job, but since she had worked so hard to get her position, she was reluctant to let it go. Besides, she wasn't sure that she could make as much money doing something else. Eventually, the stress of trying to succeed in a position for which she wasn't suited wore her down, and she quit.

Despite the fact that Tom was twenty years older than Judy, he continued to thrive in his position. The pressures of the job seemed to challenge him to do his best and he handled them with grace and exuberance. Tom found great satisfaction in his job and couldn't imagine himself doing anything else.

The difference between Tom and Judy is in the satisfaction that talent brings. Tom found nourishment for his soul through his work. Judy found herself drained and depleted. When we engage our talents, we find ourselves in the position of Tom: no matter how high the pressure goes—even when we are physically tired by it—we find contentment and challenge in our work.

RAPID LEARNING

Another reliable and important hallmark of talent is rapid learning. Where our talent leads us, we go there more quickly. Even though we may have never tried our hand at the task, it feels as if we have done it before. Our innate ability helps us to assimilate the experience with ease and we quickly gain finesse.

The phenomenon of rapid learning is something we have all experienced in ourselves or in others. Immediately we recognize this as the beginning of talent: "She's a natural." "He found his niche." "She's got a knack for it."

Slow learning, on the other hand, is a good indicator of the absence of talent. No matter how strong our yearning to do something, if we find that our progress is frustrated and slow, it's most likely not one of our talents.

The clearest example of rapid learning in my own life comes from my teenage years, when I learned to play the piano. My piano teacher, a very qualified concert pianist, struggled for years to teach me to read and play classical music. I, a willing but slow student, spent hours trying to master the works of great composers, but I progressed very slowly in my ability to read both the notes and timing of more complex piano music. Year after year went by while I labored at trying to improve my music-reading skills, with very little progress. I was definitely a slow learner.

On the weekends, however, I had great fun playing the piano and organ at the church my family attended. Since I knew many of the old hymns from early childhood, I found I could sit down and play them without music. Much to the horror of my piano teacher (who attended the same church), I found great satisfaction in "playing by ear," and I learned to do it well. In no time at all, I was using my ear as a substitute for reading music. If my piano teacher played a piece of music for me first, I worked around my weak reading skills by imitating what I had heard. Eventually, my music teacher and I agreed that teaching me to read music was not successful, and I quit the lessons. To this day, I still play the piano almost entirely by ear.

Clearly, my talent was not in reading or playing music, but in imitating notes that I heard. Playing by ear was not a struggle for me. In fact, I often felt that I was "cheating" when I would opt to play what I heard instead of the sheet music I couldn't read. My rapid, effortless learning to play by ear was a good sign of where my musical talents lay.

Although the task of the executive is entirely more complex, the same lesson holds true. When an executive takes a job that matches his talent, he quickly learns to do it well. While others may flounder in the same job for years, the executive with the talent thrives and often needs little guidance in learning the job. As a rule of thumb, any job in which you can learn the basic tasks and excel at them within a few months is a good fit with your talents. If, after three months or so, you still feel like a stranger to your job, you probably don't have the necessary potential to master the job as it currently exists.

Yearnings, satisfaction, and rapid learning are all good indications of talent. When all three are present, you can be certain that you have a natural ability to do the task at hand. While none of these things guarantees that you will be the best, they do indicate that you have found the niche *that is the best for you.*

Shaping Up a Job

At about this point in my work with executives, I usually hear something like, "It would be great if I had a job that tapped my talent, *but I don't*! What do I do?" Should you find yourself in a job that doesn't tap your talents, the situation is far from hopeless. You must shape the job to fit your strengths.

At some time or another, particularly in today's world of constantly changing organizations, you may find yourself in a job that has little relevance to your abilities. Reorganizations often create positions that aren't a good match for any of the available candidates; consequently, the company may be forced to place you in a position that doesn't fit your talents.

The first step is to find the elements of the job that you do well. And if you can't find any existing elements, look for ways in which you can expand the job in the areas of your strengths. Every job can change, so take control of that change and steer it in your direction.

There is a great deal of research evidence that shows successful executives actively *create* their jobs. Rather than allowing a mismatched position to hide their strengths, they begin to mold the job into a showcase of their finest abilities.

Take for example Dan, a compensation and benefits director for a Fortune 500 company. Dan started in human resources with his first job out of college and worked his way up through the divisional ranks to become the human resources manager of the largest division within his company. Dan had excellent working relationships with the line managers in his division and they relied upon him for workable solutions to some very sticky issues surrounding the company's labor contract. Dan was a superb negotiator.

For all his strengths, Dan wasn't particularly good with numbers, particularly when it came to compensation and benefits. For most of his career, the corporate staff determined the compensation and benefits policy, so it wasn't a problem for him. That is, it wasn't a problem until the company vice president of human resources placed him in the job of corporate compensation and benefits manager.

When Dan took over the job, he focused on the areas of his strengths: labor negotiations and relations. Since much of compensation and benefit policy originated out of labor negotiations, Dan concentrated much of his efforts on getting the best possible agreement with the labor union. As for the development of the specific pay scales and benefit packages, Dan hired several "accounting types" who were sticklers for detail and thrived on fleshing out the compensation plan.

After being in the job for a year, Dan turned his attention to negotiating with the company's health-care providers, relocation subcontractors, and temporary help agencies. Once again, he was able to forge more favorable agreements from all and trimmed a significant amount from his department's budget.

Typically, the successful compensation and benefits manager is one who understands and enjoys the intricacies of compensation tables, benefit schedules, and retirement payout projections. Dan was quite the opposite, but he was able to shape the job to meet his other strengths. As a result, he has been able to succeed in a job that initially appeared to be a mismatch with his talents.

Enlightened Delegation

The example of Dan illustrates the second point of adapting a job to meet your talents: learn to delegate your weaknesses. When a job demands that you engage in activities that are clearly not your strong suit, find a way to delegate those tasks to someone who is an expert in that area. If possible, hire capable staff members whose talents complement (as opposed to replicate) your strengths.

Frances, a San Francisco–based management consultant, is a well-known expert in the area of total quality. She has worked with a number of companies, including several multinational conglomerates, to implement their quality programs companywide. Despite her considerable expertise and education, Frances is uncomfortable with the complex statistics and data crunching required to process the survey instruments she regularly uses in her consulting work. Her solution? She hires experts, often graduate students in research or statistics, to do her statistical analysis. Her clients, who are more interested in the final reports than in the technical details of processing the data, often never know that she has managed her weakness by subcontracting out the number crunching. They are, however, very pleased with the useful data she skillfully feeds back to them.

Another poignant, if not ironic, example of delegating weaknesses was reported in January 1998 in a *Newsweek* article that chronicled the way Bill and Hillary Clinton handled the numerous crises of his presidency. The article gave detailed examples of how the President and his wife worked together, noting Hillary's role in directing crises management at the Clinton White House. "It's Bill's job to use his strengths to advance their career; it's then Hillary's to keep his weaknesses from ruining them both."[2]

Enlightened delegation is absolutely critical to the aspiring executive. Sooner or later, every executive finds himself in a situation that he is not entirely equipped to handle. In some cases, he hires staff members to help him. In others, he hires "shadow consultants" who work behind the scenes, much like presidential advisers, to keep him informed and on the right track. However it is handled, the successful executive not only soars with his strengths, he carefully delegates his weaknesses.

KNOWING WHEN TO SAY WHEN

There also may come a time when the executive must know that it is time to leave a job. When the demands of the environment absolutely require expertise she doesn't have or when the job doesn't offer sufficient opportunity for her to use her strengths, the time has come for her to move on to another position. Remaining in such a job is, at best, merely doing time, and at worst it is destroying her reputation for excellence.

One of the most public examples of an executive leaving a position for another that highlighted his strengths is when Lee Iacocca left Ford Motor Company to head Chrysler Corporation. Shortly before the move, Henry Ford II had passed over Iacocca for the chairmanship of Ford, in spite of preparing Iacocca for the position for more than a decade. Rather than cling to a job that didn't fully engage his talents, he left Ford after more than twenty years of service and took over the reins of the then troubled Chrysler Corporation. Iacocca then built a powerful management team and brought Chrysler back from the verge of failure.

Executive success starts with eliminating the fears that cloud reality, trusting our strengths as internal guides to success, and delegating our weaknesses. It is a simple formula that allows the best within us to rise to the surface and helps us achieve our highest potential.

NOTES

1. Donald Clifton and Paula Nelson, *Soar with Your Strengths* (New York: Dell Publishing, 1992).
2. Howard Fineman and Karen Breslau, "Sex, Lies and the President," *Newsweek*, January 26, 1998.

TWELVE

Stop Trying to Fix Yourself

Many executives, eager to become successful, try to do so by improving their weaknesses. They read books, they attend seminars, and they try, try, try. But try as they may, they rarely improve. Those who don't have strong "people skills" rarely improve their skills by taking the "managing relationships" or "dealing with difficult people" seminar. Those who have difficulty managing their time rarely improve by purchasing an expensive daily planner or sophisticated time management software. And those who don't have a knack for negotiating, managing conflict, empowering employees, or even general management rarely improve from attending seminars or reading books on these topics. The data is very clear: We don't improve through the remedial education of our weaknesses. We improve by unleashing the power of our strengths.

> First, to be a good leader, you must know yourself—your strengths and weaknesses.[1]
>
> Gilbert F. Amelio, Former CEO,
> National Semiconductor Corporation

In other words, focus on what you do well, and practice, practice, practice. When you engage your strengths, you invariably refine and improve them. Then, any deficits created by your inherent weaknesses diminish. We don't fix our weaknesses—we escape them through our strengths.

Time and again, I've found this to be true in my life. I am a capable consultant and writer, but a terrible marketer. When I practice being a consultant or a writer, I become better at those tasks, and despite years of trying to improve my marketing skills (and lots of personal flagellation), I haven't improved much at all. What I have discovered, however, is that the more I consult, the more knowledge and experience I gain for future clients, and the more I write, the better my writing becomes. As I practice these strengths, my clients recommend me to new clients and my books attract more readers, consequently diminishing my need to constantly promote myself. My work has become my marketing. My strengths have overcome my weaknesses.

This is NOT the same thing as sweeping your weaknesses under the rug of denial. Rather, it is the process of acknowledging and befriending those weaknesses. *Be very clear about your shortcomings, for if you don't know them, you can't know your strengths either.* When you know what you do well, you must in the same thought know what you don't do well.

Stop trying to fix yourself. Instead, befriend your weaknesses, and do what is necessary to manage them, or surround yourself with others who can compensate for them. *But spend your time and energy on your strengths.* As you do, your talents will far outweigh the weaknesses that may now seem insurmountable.

TALENT ENVY

When you focus on your weaknesses instead of your strengths, you waste precious time and energy trying to do something for which you are not suited. Rather than building on your strengths, you idolize the strengths of others and wish for yourself talent you do not possess. You may imitate your heroes, but you will never equal their performance, for they, not you, have the talent for that particular activity. The more attention you give to acquiring someone else's talent, the less you give to the talent you do have.

Not a few executives have destroyed their careers and even personal fortunes by insisting on operating outside of their talents. One of the saddest examples of this comes from

the American Revolutionary War and America's first executive officer (before there was even the presidency), Robert
Morris, Superintendent of Finance.

Morris was a highly successful shipping merchant whose
firm, Willing & Morris, became the premier trading operation
between Philadelphia and the Caribbean during the 1760s
through the 1780s. A sharp businessman with a talent for finance, Morris had successfully cornered the mid-Atlantic
market in flour by age 15 and had formed his partnership
with Thomas Willing by the tender age of 20.

Morris quickly became known throughout the struggling
American colonies as a shrewd merchant with the highest integrity. In a time when there were no banks, no stock markets,
and very few laws regulating unfair business practices, Morris
was known to be a man of his word. While accumulating a
vast fortune during very turbulent times, he also earned an
impeccable reputation, so much so that the Continental Congress voted unanimously to offer him the first executive position of the then loosely organized colonial states.

Many scholars attribute the winning of the Revolutionary War to Morris's efforts as Superintendent of Finance. At a
time when there was great resistance among the states to any
kind of taxation (remember the earlier conflict with Britain
regarding "taxation without representation"), Morris found
ways to finance the war without direct taxation. Prior to Morris's appointment, the situation was so desperate that General
Washington, who was not one to say anything he didn't
mean, threatened to disband the army unless the new nation
found a way to pay and feed the soldiers.

Within three days after taking office, Morris presented
the plan that would ultimately become the first national bank
and the first system for financing public debt. By using his
own excellent credit and reputation, he was able to secure
loans from France and other wealthy colonists to purchase
provisions for the army.

After the war, Morris returned full-time to his business
interests, which despite the hardships of the war years had
continued to prosper. In the 1790s, however, Morris began to
wander into a business territory unfamiliar to him: real estate.
Convinced, as were many at the time, that real estate was the
investment of the future, he began buying large tracts of land

in Virginia and New York. Despite George Washington and others trying to convince Morris that he didn't have the knack for making money from real estate, he persisted, purchasing a total of 8 million acres and becoming the largest landowner in the country.

Among other things, Morris had failed to realize that the import business he had created was cash-to-cash in three months. Real estate, on the other hand, required a much longer wait for profit. Also, slight fluctuations in the real estate market (wild swings in property values were common in the newly formed renegade nation) could drive an unwary real estate speculator out of business. And it was just such a price dip that caused Morris to lose his fortune and land in debtor's prison (there were no bankruptcy laws at the time). Shortly thereafter he died owing $3 million, an enormous sum for the time.

Morris, the subject of several extensive biographies around the turn of the century, was a very capable financier. His ability to create and capitalize business was unique for the time. But by all accounts, his misfortune in real estate was more than just bad luck—it was the result of a talented businessman who saw others making vast fortunes in real estate, a business for which he had neither the knack nor the experience. Ignoring his strengths, he put on the blinders of invincibility, tried to be something he wasn't, and ultimately lost it all.[2]

As the tragic case of Robert Morris illustrates, "talent envy" is utterly self-defeating. While it may be true that we can't solve a particular problem that lies in front of us right now, adopting this as an enduring attitude, as some executives do, is a sure path to failure. When you find yourself continually ill-equipped to handle a situation, it is the *situation* that must be changed, not you. Success demands that you place yourself in situations that employ your strengths. To remain in an overchallenging job, trying to convince yourself that you are invincible and that you can handle whatever is thrown at you, is very foolish. The great opera diva Maria Callas would have never succeeded as a pop singer. The golfing champion Tiger Woods would have failed as a football linebacker. And you will never reach your greatest accomplishments by dwelling on improving your weaknesses. Be consumed with what you do well, not what you wish you did well, or worse, what you cannot do.

Rust-Out

Another way in which executives fail to fulfill their talents is through nonuse. They "tread water" in positions that don't allow them to really excel, hoping that "good enough" will do the job.

Such executives allow their talents to remain rusty and undeveloped. Instead, they become minimally competent at fulfilling the expectations of others. It isn't their "strong suit," but it is what they believe is required of them. They never excel, but they don't fail, either. Rather than maximizing their strongest talents, they try to be what they think the organization expects; since they aren't using their innate potential, they do little more than get by. Their unused abilities lie dormant, and their careers suffer from talent "rust-out." What is so tragic about this scenario is that each of us has far more potential than we will likely tap in our lifetimes. When you ignore that potential, you settle for less success than you could otherwise achieve. Your success lies within your talents. There is no other way to reach your highest potential for executive success.

Pro golfer Brad Faxon is an example of this principle. In 1984, Faxon finished 124th on the money list and barely held onto his PGA card. While it was generally acknowledged that Faxon's strong suit was his skill with a wedge and a putter, he was spending most of his time trying to improve the weaker aspects of his game, namely, to hit the ball straighter and to cultivate more power in his swing. That's when noted sports psychologist, Bob Rotella, was able to convince Faxon that his focus was misplaced, encouraging him to concentrate on the strengths of his game. "You don't have to be the best driver in the world," Rotella recalls telling him, "because you've got a great short game and a great mind."

Taking Rotella's advice to heart, Faxon focused on his putting game and became even better around the greens, to the point that many considered him the best putter on the PGA tour at that time. As a result, he earned a place on two

Ryder Cup teams and, remarkably, he finished eighth on the money list in 1996. Rotella sums up Faxon's success: "He's really learned to love his game and not wish he had somebody else's."[3]

YOU CAN'T HAVE IT ALL

I really hate to share the news, but it's true: You can't have it all. You're not destined to have it all. You can't be anything you wish to be simply because you put your mind to it. Life doesn't work that way, and despite the crates of self-help books trying to sell that bill of goods, it isn't true. Instead, you are preprogrammed for a particular kind of success. Your talents predispose you to do certain things well, other things in rather mediocre fashion, and still others not at all. They define for you the path you are meant to tread.

The belief that "I can do anything if I just believe it and try hard enough" has derailed more executives than has anything else. These executives try and try, butting their heads against rock-solid walls, failing to accomplish anything productive but failing to give up. Who knows how many millions of dollars have been spent by executives trying to prove to themselves that they can do anything, despite much proof to the contrary?

These well-meaning executives remind me of my pet English bulldog, Winston. Winston loves nothing more than a good game of tug-of-war and he will hold on to his end of the rope, no matter what. Even when he has been so overpowered that his playful opponent pulls him off the floor, he sets his teeth into the rope, dangling in midair. His tenacity is endearing, but the truth is it isn't very productive. Likewise, heroic persistence in the face of likely defeat may make for great action-hero myths, but in reality—and particularly in business—it isn't fruitful. Some battles we were never meant to fight, much less win, and no amount of positive thinking and persistence will change this.

THE BUSINESS OF TALENT

When you practice your talents, the world beats a path to your door. When you give what you have to give, speak your truth, you fulfill your purpose in this world. The author Arnold Patent has said it well: "If you have a genuine need to say something, someone has a genuine need to hear it."

You err dramatically when you first try to figure out what the world wants from you, and then attempt to give that gift. If the world already knows what it needs from you, what need is there for you? Are you nothing more than a cosmic mule whose only function is to kowtow to the dictates of your environment? Are you simply an interchangeable cog in a giant machine?

Of course not. The truth is the world doesn't know what you should say or do. It doesn't know what gift you should give. Why? Because you haven't yet given it. You have something unique and precious to give. The giving of that gift in one stroke creates a need and a solution. This is the circle of life: We give our talents to the world and the world responds by giving us what we need to prosper.

The evidence of the overwhelming power of our talents is everywhere. We didn't know we needed lightbulbs until Thomas Edison gave from his talents. We didn't know how inspiring water lilies could be until Claude Monet painted them. We didn't know how computers could change our personal lives until Steve Wozniac, the cofounder of Apple Computers, showed us. Americans didn't need a precious symbol of liberty until the French gave us the Statue of Liberty, and now we can't imagine the New York harbor without it.

Economic systems that reward the expression of talent thrive, and those that do not, ultimately fail. Consider the collapse of the Soviet system of communism. Communism interrupted the cycle of talent and reward. The gain that naturally flows to individuals from pursuing their innate abilities was diverted to the state. In the Russian communist system, almost all workers were paid equally regardless of their contribution, removing the material incentive that comes from excellence. Workers were placed into jobs according to the perceived needs of the state rather than the expression of the individual. The erroneous assumption here was that the state knew what it needed from the individual.

Any organizational system that fails to allow the individual expression of talent falls into the same trap. The best executives *create* their jobs. They give to the organization whatever it is they do best. Their talent expands and changes their job descriptions. When the organization rigidly resists this and strictly dictates to all employees what they must do, it cuts itself off from its own power and eventually renders itself ineffective. We all know these organizations, and we even have a familiar word for them: bureaucracies.

So why is it that so many executives fail to focus upon and maximize their innate talents and consequently never really succeed? Why do they try to have it all instead of trying to do what they are capable of? Why is it that they are unable to completely trust the reservoir of ability inside themselves and instead waste time trying to do tasks for which they have no potential for success? If they have within themselves everything they need to reach their highest achievements and fulfillment, why do so many settle for something less?

Learn from their mistakes. Focus on your talent, and only on your talent. In the end, it will lead you to your destiny.

NOTES

1. Michael Ames, *Pathways to Success* (San Francisco: Berrett Koehler Books, 1994).
2. Daniel Gross, *Forbes Greatest Business Stories of All Time* (New York: John Wiley, 1996).
3. Holly Brubach, "Doc Rotella's Cure for the Thinking Athlete," *New York Times,* November 11, 1997.

PART THREE
POSSESSED BY PASSION

THIRTEEN

What's a Nice Kid Like You Doing in a Joint Like This?

When I coach an executive for the first time, I usually ask a question like "What is your passion in life?" And the usual response? It's a blank stare, shifting in the chair, or clearing the throat. Whatever it is, the feeling behind the response is usually the same: "I'm not really sure."

Too many of us have lost touch with our passion. We started out eager to do something and to be somebody, but somewhere down the road, it all got muddled. There were bills to pay, children to raise, jobs that turned out to be dead ends, promotions into management, lateral moves—the list is long, but with every turn we lost a piece of ourselves in the process. The more time that passes, the more irrelevant passion seems to be in our lives.

Why does this happen so easily? There are lots of reasons. The pressures of making a living, providing for your family, and gaining financial security are extremely heavy. No one in our lives is saying, "Do you really *love* what you do?" and there are plenty of people saying, "You need to pay bills, send the kids to college, and save for retirement!"

So your passion almost always loses out. What really inspires you becomes irrelevant to what you mistakenly think will sustain you. Your *experience* of life is sacrificed for your need to *secure* life.

But I'm here to sound the alarm: If you really want to achieve success, *you've got to combine passion with your talents.*

All the truly great executives had a burning passion for their businesses, and if you want to join them, you've got to rediscover yours.

Let me quickly say that passion isn't manufactured. You can't work yourself up into passion. Motivational speakers can't give you passion. Incentives and stock options can't give you passion. Your boss can't give you passion. Passion is something that comes from within you, and no one else can tell you what will give you passion.

Burnt Out and Bored

A sure sign of lost passion is burnout or boredom. There's a terrible rumor about burnout floating around out there and maybe you've heard it. It goes something like this: "My job . . . my boss . . . my company have burnt me out!" Don't believe it for a minute. No one can burn you out but you.

"Wait a minute!" you say. "Why in the world would I do something like that to myself?" I'm glad you asked that question—let's take a minute and answer it.

Think about some of the most successful and satisfied people you know. Get a good picture of them in your mind. Now, unless your experience is really limited, you're probably thinking about someone who is constantly on the go, but never seems to tire of it. Their work could be called hectic by some, but they seem to thrive on it. A hard day's work seems to give them some sort of psychic boost, not drain them.

Why don't these people get burnt out? It's really quite simple: They are doing what they love. Even though it is demanding, tiring, hectic, and fast-paced, they love it, and it is *the love of their work that sustains them.*

I remember reading stories about Sam Walton, the legendary founder of Wal-Mart. Sam was by all measures an extraordinary fellow, but what I remember most about him was that he kept what some would call a grueling schedule of visiting Wal-Mart stores around the country. It wasn't grueling to Sam; he loved to visit the stores. He was passionate about selling, and the stores were where it all happened. Several times a week (up until a few weeks before his death) he would pilot his own plane across the country, visiting the stores where he knew many of the salespeople by name.

If he didn't really love selling, Sam's job would have chewed him up in no time. But because he loved what he did, it energized him instead of draining him. That's what practicing your passion will do. So if you find yourself burnt out, run down, or bored by your job, you're in serious need of rediscovering your passion. But hold on, help is on the way.

I Never Really Decided to Be What I've Become

Another reason we sometimes loose touch with our passion is that we set our career path in stone before we were old enough to really know our passion. Think about it. How old were you when you decided what college to attend, what your major would be, or what job to take after graduation? For most of us, those were tumultuous years of self-discovery. We didn't know our passion from a hole in the ground. Everything was so new, including our emancipation from parental control. We'd never worked at a real job, and yet we made some crucial decisions that affected the rest of our careers.

What makes matters worse, the more you invest in your career path through postgraduate degrees and résumé-building jobs, the more committed you become to a career that may not fit you well as an adult. With every passing year, it becomes harder and harder to chuck it all away and start over.

Now, as an adult, your career has careened into something that is a logical progression of an illogical choice, and the result isn't too happy. You've become an expert at doing a job that you never imagined you would do. Passion? Forget it. You're more concerned about how quickly you can retire!

It's a cruel joke that our society requires us to make such crucial decisions so early in life. A recent article in the *New York Times* noted that a child as young as eleven years old needed to select a career path in order to prepare himself for admission to the right schools in that field. Imagine it! Eleven years old. For many of us, that was the age when we were still telling everyone we wanted to be a cowboy or a ballerina.

The good news is that your career path isn't as set as you

may think. People make dramatic changes in their careers every day without missing a beat. The first thing you need to do is rediscover your passion. When you do, the right career choices will be perfectly clear.

Despite what you may have been told, executive career changes often don't require any new schooling. If you don't believe me, investigate the college degrees and career paths of your company's senior executives. I'll bet you'll be shocked to find that they cover the map. A great example of this is the new chief executive at Hewlett-Packard, Carly Fiorina. What is her degree in? Medieval history and philosophy—a far cry from her very successful career in computer science. And remember Alan Greenspan and his degree from the Juilliard School of Music?

My Work Dominates My Life

When it feels like your work is dominating your life, all you want to do is escape. Run away. Do anything but what you're doing. When executives complain bitterly about their work consuming too much of their lives, it's usually for one reason: *They're allowing themselves to be controlled by work they don't love.*

When you are working from your passion, you may work many long and hard hours, but the difference is profound—*you*, not the job, are in control. The passionate drive to work comes from within you, not from a boss or the job. When you are in control of your work, you don't feel dominated. Sure, you may have deadlines to meet and customers to serve, but those pressures don't wear on your soul.

It's Not the Work—It's the People

It's easy to pin your own dissatisfaction with work on someone else. "I'd love this job if I didn't have to work with jerks all the time." Other people are easy marks for us to blame with our own shortcomings.

Arlene is a minister who was recently hired by a church that was languishing. Several previous ministers hadn't been terribly popular with the congregation and attendance had begun to shrink. Arlene had said all the right words in her interviews and impressed the congregation with her sermon delivery and operatic singing voice. Unfortunately for the church, what she didn't say was that she really didn't have a passion for ministry. She wasn't fond of visiting the sick, she found inspirations for sermons difficult to come by, and she was growing increasingly depressed. She had spent years training for the ministry, but once the newness of it all had worn off, she discovered she didn't like it very much.

Not surprisingly, attendance at the church continued to drop off. Arlene's sermons seemed increasingly stiff and dispirited. The congregation began to wonder what had happened to the seemingly dynamic person they had hired only six months earlier. In time, the revenue of the church declined to the point that all the office staff had to be laid off and expenses cut back severely.

Arlene's response to all this was to blame the congregation. When the board of directors approached her on the subject, she angrily reminded them that they weren't doing well before she arrived, so there must be something wrong with the church. They just weren't ready for her style of ministry, she claimed.

It can be painful to admit that you've lost touch with your passion, and so it was for Arlene. Instead of looking inside herself and admitting that she had lost inspiration, she struck out at the people around her. Arlene's response isn't that unusual. Any time you find an office where people are "blamestorming" (constantly trying to figure out whom to blame next) you have found a group of people who have lost their passion. They are rudderless beings, drifting from one excuse to the next.

Objectively, Arlene's situation was set up for success. The church had no mortgage on its beautiful waterfront facility and was situated in an affluent neighborhood. Ten percent of the attendees at the church services were visitors (which is a fantastic pool of potential new members). Everything pointed to a church that should be successful.

The key problem for Arlene—as is true for many executives—was lack of passion. Without a minister's passion, the church languished despite having everything it needed for success. Who knows what would have happened with a little inspiration?

This Isn't What I Thought It Would Be

I firmly believe that no one can really know a job until he or she has done it for a while. So how can you possibly know whether a job will speak to your passion until you've done it?

Somewhere down the line, many of us accepted the rule that it is "bad to change your mind." It looks flighty and flaky—terribly irresponsible. You need to know that the only way you can really discover your passion and follow it is to change your mind. And sometimes you must change it several times.

You learn the most about yourself by doing. If you want to know what your talents are, then start doing something—anything. In no time you'll begin to discover what you can and can't do well. So it is with passion. You think you could really enjoy being an artist? Try being one on weekends and see if it works for you. You think you want to be a human resources executive? Interview for an HR job and see what it is like. You'll never really know until you try.

The key to executive decision making has always been "correct, don't protect." In other words, do something and then change your mind if it doesn't work. When we protect a bad decision, we only dig a deeper hole for ourselves. It's like throwing good money after bad, and it never has a happy ending.

So if you find yourself in a job that didn't turn out to be what you thought it would be, let yourself off the hook. Learn what it is about the job that doesn't fit you well and start looking for something else. Some of the world's greatest executive résumés are filled with lateral moves made when a job didn't turn out to work well. Believe me, you'll do more harm to your career by being stifled by a job you don't enjoy and one you probably don't do all that well, either.

Bad Advice Taken Seriously

By now you're probably asking yourself, "Where did I lose my passion?" Or maybe you're wondering, like I once did: "Do I have any passion?" Not to worry; you've got lots of passion—it's just lying dormant for now. Before you can move forward, however, you've got to first look backward and find out what steered you off course in the first place. Unless you take the time to understand where things went wrong, you're likely to repeat the mistakes of the past.

The answer to your current dilemma goes back to some of the things you were taught as a child. Your parents, teachers, ministers, and other well-meaning adults passed on to you some faulty lessons about life that they, in turn, learned from their parents. On the surface, these lessons seem to be common-sense truths, but in reality, they are dangerous lies that taught you to abandon your passion. They are so insidious that I like to call them "The Six Lies That Will Ruin Your Career."

1. *Money will satisfy you.* Many of us live as if money is the only thing that matters in this world. We hang on to jobs that we hate just for the money. We move far from family and friends because of a job with a higher salary. More than a few of us have even destroyed our marriages because we were hell-bent on making money. The deep-down truth is that most of us believe that more money, perhaps just a little bit more than what we now have, will make us happy.

Money, no matter how much, doesn't satisfy. Warren Buffet, one of America's wealthiest persons, is convinced that money doesn't make anyone happier. In a recent interview with University of Washington business students, Buffet emphatically stated that what makes him happy and fulfilled is that his work is *exactly* what he wants to do. He even went so far as to say that he regularly turns down lucrative business deals when they require him to work with "people who make his stomach churn" or because they involve some business that doesn't interest him. Buffet is so convinced that money won't make anyone happier (and can make one's life appreciably more difficult), he is leaving 99% of his considerable fortune not to his family, but to society. To Buffet, this is one of the most loving things he can do for his family.

Think of the people in your life who are the most fulfilled. Are they the wealthiest people you know? Probably not. In fact, some of the most fulfilled may not have much wealth at all. If you want to be fulfilled, the objective of your life must be to follow your passion, not to amass the biggest bank account. Remember: Success is a feeling, not a possession.

2. *Hard work makes you successful.* Of all the gifts our forefathers gave us (like the Protestant work ethic), this stubborn belief is not one of the better ones. In fact, it has destroyed more lives than it has helped. Why?

Working hard at something doesn't necessarily mean that anything good will happen. For instance, if I want a swimming pool in my backyard, I can take out my shovel and dig a hole for it. Seems a bit silly, but I could do it. Or I could rent a backhoe and do the job quickly and with much less effort. Better yet, I could contract with someone who knows how to install pools and will do it far more efficiently than I can.

If I should choose to dig the pool with a shovel, I will be working very hard, but it won't be very smart. Sure, I'll be busy, busy, busy—but for what? Digging that hole will only occupy my time and keep me from pursuing my real passion (which is definitely not digging an enormous hole).

Hard work only pays off when you first do the inner work of discovering what you want to do and consequently are good at doing. When you do that, no matter how hard you work, it doesn't seem hard at all!

In many ways, hard work is like a drug. It tires you so that you don't have the energy to think about what is within you. It temporarily deadens you to the disappointment that your life isn't what you want it to be. As a result, you constantly keep yourself busy and too tired to think about what you are missing.

In my travels as an author I have met countless people who tell me they have a book they want to write, but can't find the time to do it. They're so busy making money and doing all the other projects of their lives that they are too tired at the end of the day to even think about writing. When I suggest that they might rearrange their lives, work a little less, and set aside time to indulge their passion for writing, I get a long list of excuses why that can't happen. It's really too bad, for these people will never write a book until they are willing to let go of the myth about hard work.

3. *You should never get carried away.* This deeply held belief—that something terrible will happen if we allow our emotions to express themselves through our actions—causes us to
miss much of what life has to offer. Think of all the great
people throughout history, or better yet, of people you know
who have accomplished something of meaning in their lives.
Didn't they get "carried away?"

George Washington got carried away.
Susan B. Anthony got carried away.
The Wright brothers got carried away.
Eleanor Roosevelt got carried away.
Martin Luther King, Jr., got carried away.
Ella Fitzgerald got carried away.
Jesus got carried away.
Buddha got carried away.

The list could go on and on. The point is that you never really
reach your full potential until you get "carried away." When
you allow your deepest feelings to surface and energize your
life, you find the momentum that carries you into your greatest accomplishments.

Of course, the term "carried away" is really a misnomer.
Just because you give credence to your feelings doesn't mean
that you are wildly out of control. It simply means that
you've found a dynamic source of power within yourself and
that you've allowed that power to invigorate your life. Even
when you're "carried away," you're still very much in control
of your actions.

4. *An idle mind is the devil's workshop.* Sitting quietly with
nothing to do has become a rarity in today's world. In fact,
our modern culture seems to despise quiet solitude. Quiet
time for reflection and meditation is essential to being happy.
Your mind and body require a time of quiet to rejuvenate and
refocus. Without it, you slowly deplete yourself until you
loose touch with your inner voice. You forget who you really
are and what you want out of life, and instead choose to vi-
brate with constant busyness. Your actions lose meaningful
direction, and you are adrift in the sea of your own life.

When you take the time to block out all the noise of the

outer world, you strengthen the sound of your inner voice. In those times of silent contemplation, you retune yourself to the deep meaning of your life. You are then reminded of your purpose and passion—the two essential ingredients of your own greatness.

5. *If it isn't broken, don't fix it.* Sometimes, when everything is sailing smoothly, it is time for change. Why? Because uneventful times often mean that for some reason we have stopped growing. And, like everything else in the universe, when we're not growing, we are dying. Life is a process of change, not a stagnant experience of consistency. Nothing in this world stands perfectly still. As the business writer Judith Bardwick has aptly written, there is "danger in the comfort zone." A rich life of passion is a life of constant change and growth. When you stop growing, you begin to loose touch with your passions.

6. *You must fulfill your parents' unfulfilled dream.* Most parents have grand dreams for their children. In their own way, they want the best that life has to offer for their children. Still, however well-meaning those dreams may be, they often weigh heavily upon a child, and can actually destroy his or her entire life. How? When a child (particularly a grown child) refuses to follow her own passion and, instead, tries to fulfill her parents' expectations. Many of life's major decisions, including your choices of career, your marriage partner, where you live, how much you travel, and how many children you have can be heavily influenced by your parents' expectations of you.

Each of us has our own mission in life to fulfill. Regardless of our parents' best wishes, we must—if we are to be happy and fulfilled—follow our own passions. In my workshops, I often ask the participants to write a paragraph about what their parents wanted for them. I have them title it "What I Was Supposed to Be." For many, this exercise is an incredibly moving and inspiring experience. Consider what one executive wrote:

> I was supposed to grow up and be a wealthy lawyer or doctor who in his spare time led evangelistic crusades in the remote reaches of Africa. I was supposed

to marry a lovely wife who would bear children, treat me like a prince, and revere my mother. I was supposed to live in the finest neighborhood where my parents lived (when I wasn't preaching a revival in the African jungle), attend church regularly, and visit my parents regularly, but never ask them for money or to baby-sit my children.

Despite the fact that he had spent much of his twenties trying to fulfill these expectations, he has in his forties finally broken free to become the CEO of his own consulting company. He has a very close circle of friends, has never been married, and doesn't wish to have children.

Another moving paragraph came from a sixty-year-old woman who attended another of my seminars. During a break, she came forward and said that writing the paragraph had been incredibly difficult for her. In fact, she said with tears in her eyes, she could only write one word: "invisible." That was all her parents had expected of her—to be a pleasant background in their lives. Then she said, "I've spent much of my life trying to fulfill that expectation. Only now that I am in my sixties have I realized that I really do have some talent and a great deal to offer. I don't have to be invisible." Doubtless, this woman put into words the expectations with which many female executives must deal.

Each of these false beliefs will prevent you from living a life full of passion. They say:

"Hold back."
"Fit in and don't make waves."
"Be wary of your emotions."
"Live your life to meet the expectations of others."

Like shedding an old skin, you must shed the old beliefs that have blocked you from knowing and following your passions. Those old ideas have kept you from creating the life you have always dreamed you could have. They have blocked you from unleashing your passion on your successful executive career.

FOURTEEN

Remind Me, What Does Passion Look Like?

> But I was doing what I wanted to do. Sometimes I had to change certain things so I could continue to do what I wanted to do.[1]
>
> Robert N. Noyce,
> Cofounder, Fairchild Semiconductor and Intel

THE JOURNEY IS THE REWARD

There is a huge problem with your business education. Even though we've never met, I can bet that you've been taught, like so many of us, about the importance of goals—and the basis of that principle is fundamentally wrong. The business of goal setting and attainment is taught from the first day in Business 101. "No goals, no glory." "If you don't aim for something, that's what you'll get—nothing." You can probably recite more phrases than I can, all of which are intended to drive into our brains the importance of goals.

It isn't the use of goals that is misguided, it is the idea that the process of achieving those goals is secondary to the attainment of the goal. In other words, do whatever it takes to reach the goal and you will be successful. Nothing could be more wrong.

Let me be clear. I firmly believe that goals are a critical element of good business. What I am convinced is wrong is the deeply held belief that the *goal is more important than the journey to the goal*. It's wrong for business, and it's definitely wrong for your fulfillment and ultimate happiness.

Passion is about *doing* the work, not having *completed* the work. For example, I'm always reminded of something a great editor once said: "Many unsuccessful, aspiring writers would like to have written, but hate to write." What that wise editor is saying is that success often hinges upon your love of actually doing the work, not in lusting after the rewards of having successfully completed the work. True passion is about being a connoisseur of your profession; one who savors the experience of the job. It is enjoying the journey to your goals.

> You must believe and believe passionately in yourself and your ideas . . . never let *anyone* dissuade you. Listen to advice on how to improve your endeavor but not to the naysayers.[2]
>
> Beverly Duran,
> Chairperson of the Board, Carretas, Inc.

When we focus on the goal and see our careers as nothing more than a means to ultimate success, we will lack the stamina to reach our final goal. Passion is what keeps us working day after day, pushing through failure and hardship. Passion is what keeps us committed to the path of attaining our goal.

If you want to be a great executive, you must love the daily grind of being an executive, not just all the perks that come with the job. You must love meetings, travel, conference calls, helping others solve problems, making tough decisions under pressure, and all the other things that fill most executives' time. It's certainly admirable to aspire to become a senior executive, but if you don't have a passion for the work, you'd be better off doing something else.

The truth about goals is that you never really reach them, not in most corporations, anyway. For example, let's say you work for a chain of fast-food restaurants and your goal is to open two hundred new stores this year. You may accomplish this goal, but before you open the last one, you can be assured that new goals will immediately emerge, like: Are the new stores producing adequate revenue? Are the new managers correctly trained? Who can you hire as a district manager to oversee the new stores? How can you fix the stores that aren't producing?

There's no time to savor your attainment of the goal because there are new concerns that now completely overshadow your accomplishment. After all, if the new stores aren't successful, who cares that you met the original goal? At the end of the day, the executive's work is more like a marathon of running past many mileposts along the way rather than discreet sprints to distinct finish lines. Goals are simply a target for focus, not a reward for working, and certainly not a substitute for passion.

It's Not a Job, It's a Reason to Live

This is where the rubber really meets the road. If you aspire to be a successful anything—including an executive—you've got to have the burning desire in your soul. If you think of it as just a job and a paycheck, you're doomed from the start. Any good work will require everything you have to give it, not just eight hours a day.

> Love what you do. Success requires passion.[3]
> Carly Fiorina, CEO, Hewlett-Packard

Now, I can hear all the touchy-feely types screaming, "What about balance?" Let me say this about balance. I've worked with many very successful executives, and the only balance that is truly worth having is a life driven by passion. If you balance your time with several things, none of which you truly care about, what do you have? Not happiness or fulfillment, I can assure you.

> If you love your life's work, your happiness will radiate to those you associate with. Your love of what you do can inspire many people; this encourages them to cooperate with the pursuit of your envisioned goals.[4]
> Cathy Schnaubelt Rogers,
> President, Schnaubelt Shorts, Inc.

On the other hand, if you are wholeheartedly following your passion, it consumes your life. You then have something very real and meaningful to share with the others in your life. More often than not, unhappy relationships come from one or both parties failing to find fulfillment in their lives. Whether it be your spouse, your children, or your friends, you will be better at all those relationships if you find fulfillment in your life—and it only comes from following your passion. That's what real balance is all about.

ROLLING IN DOUGH

For most of Tom Monaghan's life he's been consumed with a passion for one simple thing: selling pizza. Tom loves everything about the pizza business, from the ingredients to the smell of it baking to the challenge of delivering it hot.

Tom's story begins in 1960 when he was a college student. It was then that he and his brother Jim borrowed $900 to open a pizza parlor near the campus of Eastern Michigan University. When Tom wasn't in school, he lived at the pizza parlor, doing every task himself—from making the sauce to scrubbing the floor. His brother Jim, on the other hand, had a full-time job at the post office and spent far less time at the parlor. Eventually the disparity between their contributions led to Jim selling his half of the business to Tom, in exchange for a 1959 Volkswagen Beetle that the business had used as a delivery car. The loss of the car was a real setback for the business, but Tom was determined to make it work.

To keep the business afloat, Tom dropped out of college. Quickly he discovered that he couldn't keep working eighteen-hour days and that he needed help, so he went looking for someone who knew the pizza business. In time he discovered a man who had successfully run his own pizza delivery business and who was interested in a partnership with Tom. For the small sum of $500, Tom gave him a 50 percent stake of the business.

Tom and his partner decided to expand the business and opened two more stores and a full-service restaurant. After a couple of years, Tom discovered that his partner was taking advantage of the business, spending money on cars and property. Nevertheless, Tom remained loyal to the partner, thinking that the business needed his partner's experience.

Eventually, the partner became very ill and deep in debt to hospitals and doctors. Since their partnership was so entangled, the partner's pending bankruptcy threatened to close the business. Ultimately, it cost Tom $75,000 to pay off his partner's debts, for which he was legally responsible.

For most, that would have been the end of the road. But it wasn't for Tom. He was determined to succeed in the pizza business. The next year, while paying off the bankruptcy debts, Tom managed to make $50,000 in net profit.

All seemed to be going well, and then disaster struck again. In April 1967, a fire wiped out his anchor store, destroying $150,000 of equipment for which the insurance was only willing to pay $13,000. Amazingly, Tom was more determined than ever and found a way to finance the losses. Within a few years, not only had he recovered from the fire, the business, now operating under the name Domino's, had grown to a dozen stores and had a dozen more under development. Nearly ten years of working eighteen-hour days, seven days a week had finally paid off. Tom had the pizza business he had always wanted.

But it was too good to be true. Once again, everything went south. Tom had expanded the business too fast and accrued $1.5 million in debt. Now, Domino's faced bankruptcy, *again.* "We had over-expanded and added new stores to territories before the first stores were fully established," Tom said. "We also made the mistake of sending in untrained managers with no experience to run the new stores and over-staffed our home office."[5]

On May 1, 1970, Tom lost controlling interest in the company. The bank took over the company and kept Tom in a figurehead position of president. The new owners closed unprofitable stores and cut back on the staff. Tom's only responsibility was to run twelve corporately owned stores.

After ten months with the new ownership, Tom arranged to buy back control of Domino's in exchange for a few franchises. Once he was back at the helm, a number of his franchisees were angry about his return and filed a class action antitrust suit against Domino's. According to Tom, this was truly the lowest point in his life.

Over the following nine years, Tom refused to give in. He slowly built the business back, paying off all the old creditors. As if all this wasn't enough, he simultaneously won a trademark lawsuit brought by Domino's Sugar.

Today, Domino's is the largest home-delivery pizza business in the world. Because of his passion for the business, Tom persisted long after many would have thrown in the towel. Owning 97 percent of Domino's, Tom became one of the wealthiest self-made persons in the country.

The story of Tom Monaghan and Domino's is one of being consumed by passion. By giving himself over to his passion, he found unlimited energy that propelled him through extraordinary obstacles. Every time disaster struck and more rational voices advised him to quit, he held on to his dreams and eventually achieved them all. Tom says of this, "I feel all these setbacks were tools for me to learn from. I used them as stepping-stones and didn't see them as failures. A failure is when you stop trying and I never did that."[6]

Pizza was Tom's reason to live. For more than ten years he lived in a small apartment with nothing but a bed and kitchenette. When he traveled for business, he would often sleep in his rusty Rambler to save money for the business. Tom's passion wasn't delicate or contained. It was bold, rough, and uncontrolled. By giving himself over to this passion, he found the one source of unstoppable energy within himself that wouldn't quit until success was his.

Was Tom ever afraid of failing? You bet. Was he ever discouraged? More than once. The difference was that he refused to give in to the voice of fear. Rather than heed those misguided whispers, he allowed his passion to guide him.

THE CREATIVE WELLSPRING

Your passion is the source of your executive creativity. Without the energy of passion, the great ideas become bottled within you and are never expressed. Michael Eisner, CEO of the Walt Disney Company, talks about his belief in passion and executive creativity:

> I am so convinced that all of us can find within ourselves hidden depths and new wellsprings of creativ-

ity that a few years ago I organized a retreat for top Disney management at the Aspen Institute, which was more accustomed to hosting charettes devoted to world political issues than to the Freudian unconscious.

The first presentation at that retreat was given by a husband-wife team who teach at the Harvard Medical School. They focused on what it means for people to connect with their emotional depths. Being in connection with these depths, they suggested, is critical to releasing our most powerful and creative forces. Denying this deeper level—whether in one's life or in relationship to others—leads to something called "disconnection." In effect, people lose touch with fundamental aspects of who they are.

The result, we are told, tends to be vulnerability, fear and denial, as well as superficiality, falseness and a mistrust of intuition—all of which can get in the way of deep creative expression. I was especially struck by the point that fear of criticism and lack of acceptance is a primary reason that people so often censor their feelings and intuitions and shut down their depths.

It explains a lot about the difference between those who are truly creative and those who are somehow blocked, or limited or superficial. Put another way, going deeper has a very practical creative value. Artists produce their best and most creative work when they aren't afraid to take risks, to endure criticism or embarrassment or even failure.

To me, such risk-taking is the primary challenge not just for an artist, but for any truly creative executive.[7]

HEART POUNDING, BLOOD PUMPING

The renowned psychiatrist William Glasser, who pioneered a very successful school of psychotherapy, has stated that every human has a fundamental need for excitement. We *need* to feel our passion. Without it, we are likely to create havoc in our lives just to feel some essence of the excitement we crave.

More than a few executives derail their otherwise promising careers because they don't follow their passion and are starved for the energy that passion brings. Instead, they create all kinds of chaos through unnecessary reorganizations, conflicts, firings, and such. Their misguided search for excitement leads them to generate tension within the organization. In time, they develop a reputation as something of a troublemaker and are passed over for more important positions.

In the life and career of the executive, the need for passion is clear. We want to be passionately involved with our career—to do something with our lives that truly matters. When we tap into this deep source of strength and energy, it multiplies our efforts and catapults our careers far beyond what we could do otherwise.

NOTES

1. Robert Noyce, "Innovation: The Fruit of Success," *MIT's Technology Review*, February 1978.
2. Michael Ames, *Pathways to Success* (San Francisco: Berrett Koehler Books, 1994).
3. Carly Fiorina, "Making the Best of a Mess," *New York Times*, September 29, 1999.
4. Ames, *Pathways to Success*, 182.
5. Cynthia Kersey, *Unstoppable* (Naperville, IL: Sourcebooks, 1998).
6. Ibid.
7. Michael Eisner, "Managing a Creative Organization" (speech presented at the Executive Club of Chicago, April 19, 1996).

FIFTEEN

What Color Is
Your Passion?

> No matter how large the business grows, it is always an
> expression of personal force.[1]
>
> A. Montgomery Ward, Founder, Montgomery Ward

To help you rediscover your passion, I'd like to offer some general categories of passion that I've observed in both aspiring and successful executives. These categories are not absolute, but can help you to understand what it is that really gets you going.

MORE THAN A POWER LUNCH

The first category of executive passion is that of power. Now I know that to say one is "power hungry" isn't terribly fashionable these days, but the truth is that the need for power is a strong passion in many successful executives.

A passion for power isn't necessarily a bad thing. In fact, channeled in the right direction it can actually be very beneficial to one's career and to society at large. The passion for power is a burning desire to control one's environment, and in so doing control one's life. It is about being responsible for critical decisions, and about seeing the results of those decisions. For many, a passion for power is about making a difference in the world.

A passion for power is clearly what drives Bill Gates, the brilliant CEO and founder of Microsoft and in the late 1990s the world's richest executive. Gates was in the eighth grade in 1968, when he first sat down at the keyboard of an ASR-33 Teletype (a precursor to modern personal computers). Even in those formative years, Gates equated computer programming with power "to control everything. There's no compromise. Every line is yours and you feel good about every line. It's kind of selfish."[2]

Regardless of how you feel about Gates and his business tactics, one thing is clear: Bill Gates wants to change the world with his vision of computing. *And he wants to be the one who makes those decisions.* While we could debate at length the value of his accomplishments and the merits of Windows software (Microsoft's premier product), we must agree that Gates has changed the world—and, in many people's eyes, changed it for the better.

Another example of the passion for power also arises from the high-tech world. Charles Wang is the CEO of Computer Associates International, the largest software company after Microsoft and Oracle. Wang started out life in the most powerless position imaginable: as a refugee from China after the communist takeover in 1949. Wang and his family immigrated to New York, where they found shelter in a poverty-stricken housing project for immigrants. After a great deal of hard work and sacrifice, Wang was able to graduate from Queens College with a degree in mathematics and physics. Soon after, he went to work for a pioneering computer company.

When the opportunity arose for Wang to buy the software division of his employer, he and cofounder Russell Artzt scraped together enough cash to make the down payment on the purchase. In the years that followed, Wang was known for his relentless work ethic and cold-call selling. Today, Computer Associates thrives under the directive management style of Wang.

Charles Wang readily ascribes his unmatched passion for power to his powerless beginnings. As an impoverished immigrant he was determined to gain some control over his destiny and to make his place in the world. Wang, through his leadership of Computer Associates, now makes decisions that regularly impact the global computer industry.

A passion for power is very different from the abuses of power that often result from a fear of inadequacy or authority (see Chapters 3 and 8). Simply craving to sit in the driver's seat does not mean that you have malicious or inhumane motives. It simply means that you want the opportunity to make the important decisions and to bear the consequences of those decisions. There is no other job as well-suited to filling the need for power as that of an executive.

Give Me a Well-Oiled Machine

Another category of passions that drives some executives is the opportunity to be part of a structured, smooth-flowing environment. Huh? Believe it or not, the job of being an executive—even in today's fast-paced world—is relatively structured and secure. The higher you move up the corporate ladder, the more secure and structured your job becomes. For example, think about layoffs. What group of employees is almost always the hardest hit? Those at the bottom. Even with all the talk over the past decade of "trimming middle management," there has been no statistical evidence of this happening. In fact, most studies show that those in middle and top management positions are as secure as they have ever been.

The higher your position in the organization, the less likely you are to be fired and, even if you are, the more likely you are to get another job of equal status. Moving up the corporate ladder is without a doubt one of the best ways to secure a career.

As for structure, take a hard look at most of the executives you know. Look at what they do every day. While they may be extraordinarily busy, there is a clear rhythm and routine to what they do. Quarterly reports have to be done every three months. Site visits have to be made on a regular basis. Once inside the executive suite, the percussive regularity of the job is almost hypnotic—which has come as no small surprise to many new executives.

DEVIL IN THE DETAILS

Executive positions in "staff" departments often require great attention to detail. The heads of departments of accounting, human resources, legal affairs, and facilities, for example, spend much of their time sorting through specific policies and numbers, making sure that the organization is running according to prescribed guidelines. The executives who excel in these positions are often those who have a passion for sifting through large amounts of detail and an ability to condense the important material for presentation to their superiors.

A CONSUMMATE SALESPERSON

Some executives spend the majority of their time trying to persuade the organization to take a certain course. For example, research and development executives, among others, regularly try to influence manufacturing executives to produce a particular product. Marketing executives spend time trying to sell a particular advertising campaign to both the sales force and to other executives. Executives who flourish in these departments almost always have a passion for selling.

Of course, executive selling is a far more sophisticated and genteel activity than selling to customers, but it is selling nonetheless. An executive passion for selling is a passion for changing someone else's opinion and for influencing their decisions. It is very much about loving the "game" and trying to win by influencing others. These executives are known to lay awake at night just imagining all the ways they might sell their ideas to another executive.

CRAVING TEAM SPIRIT

Another category of passion that propels executives to the top is the desire to be part of a winning team. These executives crave the team interaction and the feeling of a closely knit group accomplishing a challenging task. Theirs is not a need to control so much as it is to be participant or coach.

Once again, we find a great example of an executive with a passion for teamwork in the field of high technology. Robert Noyce was the cofounder of Fairchild Semiconductor, Intel, and Sematech. Noyce's passion for teamwork led him to create what was considered at the time to be a radical organizational structure (the structure was so successful, it has now become commonplace in creative organizations). His idea of corporate structure was to have autonomous units that were free of centralized control. As long as it stayed within certain guidelines, each unit was allowed to pursue its own projects and goals. To coordinate all the autonomous units within the company, councils were set up to solve problems and facilitate cooperation among the units. The councils had no real power but were set up to be freewheeling discussion forums for the business units.

Success in Noyce's mind was determined by a team that was allowed to govern itself. Ultimately, his hands-off policy paid off handsomely, as the success of all three companies he founded and ran is legendary.

TROUBLESHOOTING

Troubleshooting is another passion that drives some executives. These executives are drawn to organizations that are in jeopardy, and they get their kicks by turning them around. This is usually a very risky endeavor, and these executives thrive on the adrenaline rush that comes with the risk. The worse off an organization, the sweeter their reward if they are successful.

An executive who craves troubleshooting doesn't stay in one place too long. After all, there are only so many serious problems to be solved in any organization. Once they have fixed the big issues, they quickly get bored with the daily routine of running a healthy department or company. In order to follow their passion they must either move to another troubled organization or—and this is what most do—they must continue to grow their organizations so that they can troubleshoot the inevitable difficulties that come with expanding a business.

There are many great examples of this kind of executive,

and surely at the top of the list is Lawrence Bossidy. Bossidy is currently the CEO of AlliedSignal. Prior to that, Bossidy worked his way up the corporate ladder under the leadership of Jack Welch at General Electric (GE), eventually becoming Welch's number two man. While at GE, Bossidy turned around numerous departments that had fallen into the sluggish bureaucracy that GE had become before Welch took over. Much of Welch's success at GE was clearly attributable to Lawrence Bossidy.

When Bossidy took over AlliedSignal, it was a loose federation of many divisions that produced a little of everything, from aerospace to auto parts. Bossidy was hired to turn around the mature and ailing company. Almost immediately he began troubleshooting the outdated organizational processes and refocused the company on beating its competitors to market. Within a few years, Bossidy had completely restructured and invigorated a company, a task that many had thought was impossible.

Today, Bossidy focuses on solving the problems associated with growing a business as complex as AlliedSignal. Because the twenty-plus businesses that make up AlliedSignal are so diverse, there is no shortage of challenges for him to tackle. Undoubtedly, he wouldn't thrive on anything less.

WHAT DRIVES YOU?

Now that we've looked at some of the categories of executive passion, it's time for you to ask, "What really excites me about business?" Take a long, hard look at yourself. What kind of job or type of task gets you out of bed in the morning with anticipation? The sooner you take the time to really understand where your passion lies and then stay true to it, the sooner you will avoid many of the career pitfalls that other aspiring executives hit. They take the first job that looks like a promotion and then find they don't have the passion to become a champion.

But you don't have to take the first promotion that comes your way. In fact, the only promotion you should ever take is one that appeals to longings of your heart. If you will take this advice and always remain faithful to your passion, the promotions that will take you to the top will land in your lap—*You can count on it.*

NOTES

1. Montgomery A. Ward, *Personality in Business* (New York: The System Company, 1910).
2. Peter Krass, *The Book of Leadership Wisdom* (New York: John Wiley, 1998).

PART FOUR
ACTION IS THE ANTIDOTE TO FEAR

SIXTEEN

How to Get Lucky

At this point, it's time to start pulling it all together. You've looked at the voices of fear that hold you back, and carefully considered your talent and your passion. Now it's time for action.

It's really helpful to remember one important thing: *the whole point of fear is to keep you from acting.* That's what fear does to you—it keeps you stuck, or worse, puts you in retreat. The bottom line of everything I've told you until now is *action.* Practicing your talent requires *action.* Following your passion requires *action.* Overcoming the bonds of fear requires *action.* In case I haven't said it enough, here it is again: YOU'VE GOT TO TAKE ACTION.

In case you're still worried about heading in the wrong direction, you've got to remember that *even action in the wrong direction is helpful.* It's really true. Even when you do all the wrong things, you are moving forward. How? Because you're learning all the way and you won't make those mistakes again. Had you sat back and contemplated your navel, you would have never learned that lesson and would be one step behind where you are now.

> Being a visionary isn't enough. Rather, our future leaders must be willing to put their ideas into action, challenge old assumptions and make changes to improve performance.[1]
>
> John Bryson, CEO,
> Southern California Edison Company

Action is the only way to raise confidence in your talents. Every time you fail to do something because of fear, your confidence slips a notch or two. You only give yourself one more piece of evidence why you shouldn't take action in the future. When you face down your fear and step up to the plate, you raise your confidence a notch. Even when you strike out, your confidence has been raised because you were able to take that step. Every executive feels fear, but the only ones who are defeated by it are the ones who fail to act. Action is the only way to get lucky. If you never ask the question, you'll never get a "yes." If you never take the risk, you'll never get the payout. If you never look for the treasure, you'll certainly never find it. If you never practice your talents, you will never become a superstar.

THROWING OUT THE BABY

There are shelves of books and tapes for sale today promising that if you quit your job and jump into what you've always dreamed of doing, your life will be filled with riches.

Sorry, but it ain't so. I wish it were true, but it just isn't. Effectively taking action doesn't mean that you must take dramatic steps—those are most certainly fraught with danger. It means taking a manageable step with what you know right now. In time those manageable steps will add up to something big. But first you've got to start the forward motion.

Consider, for example, the story of chemist Spencer Silver at 3M Corporation. In 1978 he developed an adhesive that would stick to a surface but would not permanently adhere to it. With a little ingenuity, he applied the adhesive to scratch paper in order to stick notes on lab equipment. Quickly he realized he had just developed a marketable product.

The executives at 3M were less than enthusiastic, wondering who would pay a buck for a pad of scratch paper. Nevertheless, Silver persisted within the company, and after six years of transfers, closed doors, and failed marketing tests his product made it to the market. Today, no businessperson's desk is without it: 3M Post-it® notes.[2]

What's critical to Spencer Silver's success is key to the

success of thousands of other executives like him. He didn't quit his job, borrow a million dollars, and try to sell the stacks of notepaper himself. No, he took small steps every day within the company, slowly finding people to back his idea and create the product. Ultimately, his persistence created a legendary career and great personal success.

More recently, consider the phenomenal resurgence of the nostalgia-inspiring Volkswagen Beetle. The designer, J. Mays, is a native of Maysville (named for an ancestor), Oklahoma, and he grew up playing on the Go-Kart track in town. In college, Mays studied commercial drawing and journalism, although he continued to be obsessed with automobiles. Shortly after graduation he discovered that "somebody would actually pay me money to draw cars." That's when he took a job with Audi-Volkswagen. For fourteen years he worked there, slowly working his way up the corporate ladder, all the time trying to sell the idea of returning to the beautiful designs of cars in previous decades—the ones he had grown up admiring. Finally, in the mid-1990s he was given a chance to put his career on the line and redesign the classic VW Beetle. The rest, of course, is history, visible today on every street in America. The car was a booming success.

Mays didn't change his career overnight. At the same time, he never relinquished his passion for beautifully designed cars, even in the 1980s, when most experts agree that car design was more utilitarian than aesthetic. What Mays did is what you can do: Take little steps every time an opportunity presents itself. Persistent shuffling through the corporate structure is the only sure way to success.[3]

ACTION BREEDS NEW IDEAS

The real beauty of taking action is that it is infectious. By that I mean that action always inspires new and better ideas. Even when you think you've created a failure, it isn't that at all. It's what I call "opportunities despite the outcome," which means that no matter what the result, new opportunities pop up that you couldn't have foreseen had you not taken action.

Remember Spencer Silver and the Post-it Notes adhesive? What Silver was originally looking for was a *good* adhesive, not one that was weak. By his original intent, the discovery was a failure, but it was a failure that contained great opportunities to be exploited. Even though the adhesive failed to adhere strongly, its properties were valuable because they answered a completely different need.

Call it serendipity or making lemonade out of lemons, if you must. Whatever the label, action always opens new doors that cannot be anticipated. That's why armchair executives never succeed. They spend so much time in analysis that they fail to act and miss out on great opportunities. The real key is to make your best estimate and then move.

BREAKING THE PARALYSIS

Over the years I've worked with several well-known and respected high-technology firms. As you might imagine, these companies are staffed with some of the best and brightest people around, creating a highly competitive and intellectually challenging culture within these organizations. The challenges and the stakes are both very high, so taking action can be risky.

In these organizations, it's also quite common for a certain cynicism to take hold. Since it is safer to criticize someone else than to take action, people retreat into the safety of criticizing the actions of others rather than doing something to solve the problems at hand. In the extreme, some employees never do anything—they structure their jobs around full-time criticism.

Certainly, criticism is necessary, but this kind of organizational culture is extremely dysfunctional and based on fear. Those who stick their necks out bear the very real risk of having their heads chopped off. All it takes is for one person to take a meaningful risk, fail, and then be skewered on the organizational barbecue, and everyone else will pull back and begin giving in to fear.

In such an environment, it is easy to avoid taking any action. Abraham Lincoln is credited with saying: "It's better to be quiet and thought a fool than to open your mouth and remove all doubt." Likewise, it is possible to maintain the illusion of being the perfect executive if you never put yourself on the line. Even in highly competitive corporate cultures, your career is always better served by taking action. Even if you make a mistake that costs you your job, in the long run you will go further by always choosing the path of action.

Even in stumbling you are moving forward, although that might be difficult to see at the moment it is happening. When you hold back and refuse to move, you only prolong the inevitable. While you stand there surveying the treacherous landscape before you, your fears only grow greater, making that first step even more difficult. Your fear holds you back from achieving your best.

It's been called "beginner's luck." Others have called it "blind stupidity." Whatever label you choose, the wisdom remains the same: *When you put yourself in action, you don't have time to be afraid.*

Once a colleague of mine took the red-eye to London for an important early morning business meeting. When he returned, I asked if he was jet lagged during the all-day meeting. "Was I supposed to be?" he replied. "I guess I haven't read that book yet." His point is well taken: If you don't spend time and energy on the fear, you eliminate a great deal of the problem from the start.

As we have seen, the outcome of all fear is usually retreat or inactivity. If you're moving forward, you can't do either of those things. Action is a strong antidote to fear.

Luck Only Happens When You're in Action

That's why successful executives always appear to have "charmed" careers. It isn't anything mysterious or complicated. They act on the urgings of their talent. Even when they fail, they're lucky.

The truth is that inside you is an animal with great instincts. You know how to survive in a world of people because it's in our human genes. After all, that's what the corporate game really is—a world of people interacting. You've got some bit of something that all those other players need. It's up to you whether you'll develop and exploit it. Why not start now?

NOTES

1. Michael Ames, *Pathways to Success* (San Francisco: Berrett Koehler Books, 1994).
2. P. Ranganath Nayak and John Ketteringham, *Breakthroughs* (San Diego: Pfieffer & Company, 1994).
3. Jim McCraw, "Six Hot Designers Make Cars Look Cool Again; Father of Reborn Beetle Gets a Big Family at Ford," *New York Times*, October 21, 1998.

SEVENTEEN

What's Stopping You?

$\mathbf{O}$ur discussion of fear won't be complete without looking at some of the more devious ways it influences us to succumb to inaction. Psychologists have long labeled this more insidious, almost unconscious, form of fear as "resistance." Even though this kind of fear isn't as readily apparent as what we discussed earlier, it is every bit as strong.

Resistance appears as more of an excuse than fear. It parades through our lives as a legitimate reason why we should excuse ourselves from doing what will make us truly successful executives. But take a closer look. Resistance isn't really legitimate. It is nothing more than sophisticated self-sabotage.

I'M TOO BUSY

Anyone who has ever done management consulting knows this one really well. Basically it's stated something like this: "I'm too busy at the moment doing what isn't working to talk about how I might change and give another method a try." To tell you the truth, I'm guilty of using this one, and I'll bet you've given it a try before, too.

Anyone in business today is extraordinarily busy, and there is nothing inherently wrong with that. But busyness can sometimes be used as a form of denial, particularly for the executive. By filling your time with high-involvement activities, extra travel, and frequent meetings, you leave little time to worry about what your career isn't giving you. By the time you fall into bed at night, there is no more time or energy to think about what truly matters. In the morning, you'll rise and repeat the story again.

In today's culture, a hectic schedule is taken to mean that you are important. The fact that people are calling your mobile phone, paging you, and sending you volumes of e-mails is evidence that you are needed. Not a few executives would panic if all the clamor around them went silent.

Today's most successful executives force themselves to take time for quiet contemplation. There is some place, whether it is alone on the golf course, driving to work or quietly sitting at their desk with the door shut, where they can reflect on the direction of their careers and their lives.

A time of contemplation isn't a luxury—it is a necessity for success. You *must* have some time each day to meditate on the activities of that day. Otherwise you will be swept along on the prevailing current of your environment, much like a rudderless ship in a storm.

If you want to achieve your highest potential as an executive, you must regularly give yourself the space to think about your talents and your passion. Ask yourself, "Am I enjoying what I do? How could I enjoy it more? What did I do well today? How can I do more of it?" These are extremely important questions that demand an honest answer. Go ahead—try them right now. Take ten minutes and seriously ponder these questions. The answers will change your career.

I Don't Have the Energy

Closely related to the resistance of being too busy is that of being too tired. The first surefire sign of an executive in trouble is complaints of exhaustion.

A colleague of mine likes to say that exhaustion isn't from exertion, it's from a lack of inspiration. And he is right. Successful executives thrive in positions that would drain someone of lesser talent for that job. They are *energized* by what they do.

If you find yourself often complaining about being too tired, it's a critical time for you to take a hard look at what you are doing. Why is this job draining you? Are you really equipped to do the job well? What happened to your passion?

When your job matches your talent and passion, you will discover that even when you are physically tired, your mental state is one of exhilaration. That kind of job feeds you rather than drains you. If that's not the kind of job you have, it's time to ask yourself: "Why not?"

THAT'S NOT MY STYLE

There has been a great deal of talk about management "styles" in the last decade. Unfortunately, some executives who are unwilling to change blame their closed-mindedness on their style. "Well, that's just not my style!" they say when asked to change.

There is a huge difference between being true to your talents and refusing to get along with others. You should never try to do a job for which you have little talent, even when others expect you to do that job. On the other hand, your success depends on your willingness to learn from and work with those around you.

No matter what your talents, you can control the way you choose to present those talents. You don't have to be a "people person" to get along with people. In fact, some of the most successful CEO's I've worked with are not "people persons," yet they get along splendidly with virtually everyone they meet.

How can this be? They are respectful and authentic. Even the most focused, number-driven, high-strung executives can take the time to simply acknowledge the humanity of others. They don't have to be touchy-feely or ask about the wife and kids. They simply respect the dignity of everyone with whom they work. Other people sense this almost immediately, and even though these executives may have gruff exteriors, they are able to create strong working relationships.

I DON'T REALLY WANT TO CHANGE THAT BADLY

This resistance falls under the heading: "If it isn't broken, don't fix it." It is a huge mistake. Just because things are going OK now doesn't mean that there isn't a good reason for you to keep following your talents. As I stated in the preface to this book, I operated this way for a long time. Because I had achieved some success at what I was doing, it was very tempting to continue doing it, even though I thoroughly disliked it. I was making a great paycheck and getting promotions, so why change?

Ultimately, following this path, I would have sold myself short. Not only would I have spent my career being miserable, I would have never moved on to something that would bring me even greater and lasting success. My talents would have languished and I would have eventually found myself playing the role of the bored bureaucrat. That's not exactly what I had hoped my career would be—and I'll bet it isn't what you want either.

Sometimes moderate success can be as dangerous as an addictive drug. It lulls us into inactivity while our career dies a slow death. The occasional taste of success keeps us partially content and fools us into settling for something far less than what we deserve.

I'VE GOT MORE IMPORTANT THINGS TO DO

Think about this carefully. What is more important than your own fulfillment? If you spend your life doing things that other people see as "important" but that mean little to you, what have you really accomplished? When you are fulfilled by your work, you are a better marriage partner, parent, and friend. People who are truly passionate about their work share that passion with all the other people in their lives.

The most important thing in your career, whether you are an aspiring executive, artist, writer, minister, or whatever you choose, is to trust your instincts. They have been given to you for a very good reason, so listen to them. They're guiding you to create the most important and meaningful life you can possibly imagine. Nothing else matters.

Resistance comes into your life in many forms, and I wish I could promise that once overcome it never comes back, but I can't. The best you can do is stay vigilant to all the resistance that bubbles up from the dark corners of your mind. By fanatically refusing to relinquish your gifts, you can brush aside any challenges—especially the ones you create for yourself.

PART FIVE

Forged in the Fire: The Passages of a Fearless Executive

When we step back and look at the careers of successful executives, we see three distinct phases or *passages* through which they passed on their journeys to fulfill their executive potential. Each of these passages was marked by distinct struggles and lessons; only when the lessons were learned did the executive successfully move on to the next passage.

In the following section, we take a close look at each of these passages in the successful executive's career.

EIGHTEEN

Passage One: Every Executive Starts in the Mailroom

It's true, we all start in the mailroom on our way to the top. OK, maybe not the *real* mailroom, but it is extremely rare that even the most talented people start in an interesting and challenging job. The metaphorical mailroom is an entry job that serves one very important purpose in your career: It gives you the opportunity to discover your talent and passion.

Whether you come from an Ivy League advantage or straight from high school, the function of the first executive passage is always about discovering your strengths. That's why those first jobs are so bland. They create a space where you can discover yourself and do the least amount of damage.

Why *must* you pass through the mailroom? It's really quite simple. The everyday, day-in and day-out grind of working a job is very different from studying, fantasizing, or watching a job from afar. The experience of *doing* a job tells you more than you could ever learn about yourself from any other source. The mailroom gives you an opportunity to try a number of tasks without great risk.

THE METAPHORICAL MAILROOM

Mailroom jobs come in all shapes and titles, such as executive assistant (glorified secretary), junior executive (a half step above glorified secretary), or anything with the word "coordinator" or "trainee" in it. Every organization has its unique mailroom positions.

You may be wondering why we are talking about such low-level jobs when you have probably long since advanced beyond these entry-level positions. Well, there's a good reason—and you need to know it. The mailroom is where you must clearly identify your talent and passions—what you do well and what you enjoy doing. If you don't learn this lesson in the mailroom, you may move forward but you will continually be undermined until you discover these two basic truths about yourself. The mailroom experience is absolutely critical to your career success.

One of the great pitfalls in the mailroom is impatience, which is only exacerbated by arrogance. "Why should I do a job that is beneath me?" "I didn't go to college to do this." "I want a job with a *real* future." "This stuff bores me." When your hunger for success overshadows your willingness to learn, you sabotage yourself before your career ever really starts. Not a few potentially great executives have stunted their careers because they refused to learn from the mailroom experience.

Fashion Isn't Always Glamorous

John had his heart set on becoming a fashion buyer for a stylish retailer. After completing design school, he was lucky to land an entry job at one of America's most fashionable department stores. The position was titled "assistant analyst" and consisted of everything from typing the purchase orders dictated by the buyer to collecting sales numbers for the department's retail analyst. The job was anything but cool and fashionable (which is what John had imagined a buyer's position would be).

John had studied fashion merchandising and was considered to be quite talented by his instructors, and so he began to feel that his job was beneath him. After all, this wasn't what he wanted to do. He quit that job after a year and found another job at a less fashionable retailer.

After passing through a series of jobs and companies, John finally landed a position as a buyer with a mass-market discount retailer. The company's focus was on volume sales and it expected buyers to purchase merchandise cheaply that could be sold in large quantities. John hated this retail philosophy and fought it every way he could. After a few years of lackluster sales in his department (after all, the customers were shopping for bargains, not for the high-fashion items that John put on the racks), John was fired. Soured on his retail experience, John went to work for a temporary employment agency.

Had John been willing to pass through the mailroom and learn what it had to teach, he would have discovered some very important truths. First, the retail buyer's position is more about quantities, dollars, and analysis than it is about fashion and aesthetics (which were John's interests). Second, he would have learned that if he still wanted to be a buyer, he would need to work for a company that would allow him to focus on new products and would provide him with a strong analyst to handle all of the number crunching. Finally, John may have learned that where his talents would really shine was in the product development department rather than in a buyer's job. Product developers traveled the world looking for new sources for merchandise and fashion—a perfect fit with John's interests and passions. Had he allowed the mailroom to teach him that, John would have had a good chance of excelling in the fashion industry.

WHY IS THIS HAPPENING TO ME—AGAIN?

The funny thing about the mailroom lessons is that they keep coming back to haunt you when you fail to learn them. In John's case, every job kept trying to teach him the same lesson that he was stubbornly unwilling to learn. Finally he landed in the greatest mailroom of all—a temporary employment agency that circulates you from job to job and company to company every few weeks. What better opportunity could there be for John to discover his talents and passion?

Take a minute and think about your mailroom experiences. What were they trying to teach you about yourself?

What did you learn? Are you still circling back through mail-room after mailroom?

You will never move on to the next passages on your way to becoming a successful executive until you navigate the mailroom. The lessons are simple but ever so profound. What are your strengths? What do you really enjoy doing?

NINETEEN

Passage Two: Proving Ground

Once you've made your way through the mailroom and have begun to discover your talents, you enter into the proving ground passage. The proving ground is where you become a specialist. The proving ground passage is all about refining your talents and overcoming your fears. Here you learn how to trust your talents to lead you down successful paths and how to silence the fears that may be holding you back from giving 100 percent.

In much of the world's great literature the desert is a metaphorical symbol for the proving ground passage. The desert is a barren and difficult place, where survival requires that you use your instincts and *prove* yourself fit. Every great executive must successfully pass through the desert at some point in his or her career.

Your passage through the desert is somewhat difficult, although it has its joys, too. In the desert, successes are often far apart, but they are all the more rewarding when they are achieved. The desert period is filled with struggle that accentuates the few rewards that come your way. Perhaps the most disconcerting experience of the desert is that it highlights your shortcomings and forces you to examine your life and career carefully. The good news is that on the other side of the desert comes a pinnacle experience: *You have confronted your fears and learned how to trust the wisdom of your talents.* The end result makes all the sacrifice worthwhile.

THE RIGHT STUFF?

While you're in the desert, things can seem pretty rough. The desert seems to say to you, "Let's see if you really have what it takes." It forces you to take yourself very seriously.

Recently, I attended a leadership conference where I met with several friends and colleagues who were also in attendance. After one of the daylong sessions, we all went out to dinner to discuss the day's events and to get caught up on old friendships. As we chatted about what was happening in each of our lives, one of my friends, Andrea, who had recently left a large employer and started her own consulting firm, told us all about the financial unpredictability of starting her new business. Since most of us at the table were self-employed, we knew instantly of the fears she was relating—it is something we all had been through at least once. Finally, she said laughingly, "I just wish I had a million dollars. That would solve all my problems."

Almost instantly, another colleague at the table said to her, "Andrea, I just sold my business for over a million dollars and I can tell you with confidence, money doesn't solve all the problems. Whether you have plenty of money or are just struggling to get by, the issues are the very same."

When money is scarce and the future unclear, it seems that there is a legitimate reason to wallow in your fear. You're close to the edge—in fact, at times you can even see over the cliff to the murky waters below. It's tempting to think that more money, power, or prestige will solve all your problems. And yet this vulnerable time in your life is when you must—if you are to pass through the difficulty and flourish—confront and overwhelm your fears.

No amount of money, power, or prestige will eliminate your fears. Quite the contrary, having more of these things only brings greater fear. You worry that you will lose your money, be thrown out of power, or have your reputation irrevocably destroyed. The only antidote to fear is complete trust in your talents. This is the lesson of the desert in your life.

THE HERO GOES TO THE DESERT

There are many stories in mythology about confronting fear in the desert of our lives. Joseph Campbell, in his writings about mythological heroes, notes that almost all the great mythological figures first retreated and confronted fear before going on to greatness. He writes:

> The usual pattern is, first, of a break away or departure from the local social order and context; next, a long, deep retreat inward and backward, backward as it were, in time, and inward, deep into the psyche; a chaotic series of encounters there, darkly terrifying experiences, and presently encounters of a centering kind, fulfilling, harmonizing, giving new courage; and then finally, in such fortunate cases, a return journey of rebirth to life. And that is the universal formula: (1) separation, (2) initiation, and (3) return.[1]

In the Judeo-Christian myths (I use the word "myth" not as a judgment about the validity of the events, but to highlight the important symbolism contained within the story), confrontations usually happen in the desert. It is precisely in that place—the desert—where your fears manifest themselves and where you must overcome them if you are to move out of the desert onto higher ground.

According to the Hebrew stories, Moses, after being dethroned and cast out of Egypt, wandered in the desert for many years. He dwelt among the nomadic tribes of Midian and passed the time as a shepherd, a very humble existence compared to the royal office he had held alongside the Pharaoh, ruler of Egypt.

It was during Moses's time in the desert that he came face-to-face with his fears. The King James Version says: "And Moses hid his face; for he was afraid to look upon God."[2]

Then, God said to Moses, "Come now therefore, and I will send thee unto Pharaoh, that thou mayest bring forth my people the children of Israel out of Egypt." Once again, we see Moses's fear resurface: "And Moses said unto God, 'Who am I, that I should go unto Pharaoh, and that I should bring forth the children of Israel out of Egypt?'"

Then, later in the account Moses continues voicing his fear: "But behold, they will not believe me, nor hearken unto my voice: for they will say, The Lord hath not appeared unto thee." Further he adds: "O my Lord, I am not eloquent, neither heretofore, nor since thou hast spoken unto thy servant: but I am slow of speech, and of a slow tongue."

It was in the desert, undeniably the lowest point of Moses's life, that he had to conquer these fears before he could become one of the greatest leaders of the Hebrew people. Only after he silenced these fears within himself was he able to trust the power of his destiny.

What we learn from the powerful symbolism in this story is the paradox of conquering fear. It is when you are vulnerable, the most susceptible to the illogic of fear, that you must resist the temptation to indulge in that fear. When the chips are down and you are facing your most difficult challenges, this is your crucial moment when you must deny fear a stranglehold on your talent. But it is precisely at this "desert" point in your life that you must wrestle with your fears if you are to progress beyond them and fulfill your calling.

It is easy to think, "Once I have arrived, made my fortune and climbed to the top, that's when I won't be afraid of anything." Sadly, that's nothing but a con. You must first conquer your fears if you are to move on to your highest executive potential.

The most beautiful part of the myth of Moses in the desert isn't his fear, but how he conquered it. The writer of Exodus illustrates this with a conversation between God and Moses: "What is that in thine hand? And he said, A rod. And he said, Cast it on the ground. And he cast it on the ground, and it became a serpent; and Moses fled from before it. And the Lord said to Moses, Put forth thine hand, and take it by the tail. And he put forth his hand, and caught it, and it became a rod in his hand: That they may believe that the Lord God of their fathers, the God of Abraham, the God of Isaac, and the God of Jacob, hath appeared unto thee."[3]

What Moses held in his hand was the vehicle for the wondrous miracles that conquered the most powerful nation in the known world. It was nothing more than his meager shepherd's rod, something he carried with him every day.

So it is with you. You must overcome your fears to discover the wonderful tools you have within. It is your rod—the talent you carry with you every day—that is the genesis of your own greatness. Once you journey into the desert and confront the fear that holds you back, you can learn to use that simple, ordinary rod to accomplish extraordinary feats.

OUT OF THE DESERT

The stories of successful executives who struggled through the desert before they found their niche in business are numerous. Consider the story of IBM chief, Lou Gerstner.

In 1993, Lou Gerstner was the first outsider to be named the head of IBM. In the five years that followed, Gerstner brought the company that once epitomized "blue-chip" back from the edge of disaster. By 1999, his brash management of the company had increased IBM's market value by more than $40 billion.

But things weren't always so rosy during Gerstner's career. After graduating from Harvard Business School, he went to work for the venerable consulting firm McKinsey and Company. At McKinsey, he skyrocketed to the top, becoming the firm's youngest principal at age 28 and one of its youngest directors at age 33. In 1978, Gerstner left McKinsey to join American Express, one of the consulting accounts he had handled. And that's when things began to slow down.

At American Express, Gerstner headed up the charge-card division, which had already begun losing ground to the revolving credit of competing cards. He was able to make some changes and realize small successes, but the long-standing corporate culture and the public image of the "tiffany" card proved to be extraordinarily frustrating for him. In addition, the company acquired Shearson in 1981, and the onslaught of new executives put even more distance between Gerstner and the top position, which he had been promised when he was hired. For much of the 1980s, Gerstner struggled, but he was unable to realize the success he hoped for. Eventually, he was passed over for the presidential office. In 1987, he made a bid to become CEO of the then floundering United Airlines, but he was turned down flat. According to insiders at United, there wasn't enough confidence in his ability to turn the company around.

By 1989, eager to jump ship, he took the head job at RJR Nabisco after giving one day's notice at American Express.

Once again, he found himself in a company where his hands were tied. RJR was saddled with debt after a $25 billion leveraged buyout, leaving little room for capital expansion. To make matters worse, RJR's arch rival Philip Morris slashed the price of its Marlboro cigarettes, creating a price war that ravaged RJR's profits and bled its stock price.

What is significant about Gerstner's time at American Express and RJR is that during those years he was not known as the golden boy he had been at McKinsey, nor as the brilliant CEO he is today. Those years were tough, filled with both personal and corporate conflicts.

As a result, however, Gerstner galvanized a management style that is uniquely his own and seems to be just what IBM needs. He cares little for textbook style management. He is direct, strategic, and focused. He doesn't spend time socializing with other executives and he rarely "networks" among colleagues. He's not given to the traditional pat-on-the back, preferring to reward good performance with healthy bonuses instead of flowery words. Other CEOs report him to be brilliant, but terribly deficient at selling himself or his company's product. Gerstner is nothing like the traditional blue suits at Big Blue. Nevertheless, almost everyone agrees that he is just what IBM needs.

During those "desert" years before IBM, Gerstner learned to rely on the talents that are now the backbone of his phenomenal success. It was then that he learned his trademark confidence and ability to make the most difficult decisions without fear. From the desert he emerged, prepared for the crowning task of his career. Despite the fact that many, both inside and out of IBM, initially doubted his ability, the desert had prepared him perfectly for the job.

As was true for Gerstner, the desert teaches you that only one thing creates success: a hard-as-nails confidence in your own ability. Regardless of what others might think, you must follow your mission in life. When you fulfill that calling, you will succeed. Not until you learn this lesson are you ready to leave the desert, and only then can you achieve your greatest potential. Otherwise, you may wander through a mediocre career, never fulfilling your dreams or accomplishing much of real meaning.

But it's not just those who are destined for the corporate

hall of fame that must go through a desert period. No matter what your level or contribution to business, to be the most effective, you must see yourself successfully through the dry spells.

The desert of our lives appears desolate and unmerciful. We struggle with the challenges it presents and with the fear those challenges bring up in us. Not until we are willing to move past the fear and trust ourselves are we able to emerge from the desert, ready and equipped for the mission of our lives.

NOTES

1. Joseph Campbell, *Myths to Live By* (New York: Viking Penguin, 1972).
2. Exod. 3 and 4, King James Version.
3. Exod. 4:1–4, King James Version.

TWENTY

Passage Three: The Fearless Executive

The crowning passage of an executive's career isn't merely the absence of fear; it is an entirely different style of leadership. Once the unfounded fears are silenced, executives are no longer threatened by many of the things that earlier in their career would have propelled them to action.

It no longer becomes important to silence and conquer peer rivals in the company. It is no longer imperative to exert heavy-handed control over every detail of the work. Employees can be trusted to handle their jobs. In short, the fearless executive becomes confident, powerful, decisive, and empowering.

This is what you become when you learn to completely trust your talents and follow your passion. You can clearly see your internal compass, and the path before you is mapped. Whatever happens, you know how to handle it. There is little that can shake your confidence.

This is the passage of the fearless executive; confidence and courage are its hallmarks. You know what you can handle and how to handle it. You know what you aren't equipped to handle, and you place that in more capable hands. You know what you want and you go after it.

There is an air about you, an energy that attracts respect and loyalty. Others are naturally drawn to you and willing to allow you to lead. To others you seem courageous, but you know you are only doing what comes naturally. You have become a fearless executive.

FINDING YOUR CONFIDENCE

You cannot make yourself confident. Rather, you become confident after mastering fear. Confidence is not something magical that gives you special powers over your adversaries, but rather it is the true essence of every human being, although it is often hidden by the veil of fear. When that dark curtain is raised, courage is the waking state of humanity.

When you are no longer controlled by fear, you live by your values—no matter what the cost. You stand up for your beliefs. You no longer tolerate the oppression of others or yourself. Life matters to you. This is real confidence.

All too often we convince ourselves that courage is a separate gift, a godlike quality that is bestowed on the great few. The courageous leaders are the ones who will conquer for us! They will lead our company through troubled times! They will shoulder the risk of growth and innovation! They will determine our path!

But this thinking is nothing more than a rationalization, a convenient excuse for wallowing in our own fear. There is no magical, mystical badge of confidence that some have and others do not. We all have courage. It is a matter of choice whether we are willing to confront our fears and wholly be ourselves to the world around us. This is the courageous leader within us all, waiting to be rediscovered.

Like the Cowardly Lion in *The Wizard of Oz,* many executives live under the illusion that they must wait for that special day when courage (confidence) is given to them. "One day, I'll be confident enough to speak my mind and follow my truth," they tell themselves.

Sadly, the executive who waits for a surge of confidence will wait forever. Executive confidence does not conquer fear; fear, once conquered, gives rise to confidence. The first task is to confront the irrational fears that blind and limit you. When you are able to feel the fear and move past it, then you find the power of confidence within yourself.

When an executive enters the passage of fearlessness, several distinct characteristics emerge. In the following sections, we'll take a look at the most important of these.

ENDING THE REIGN OF TERROR

The fearless executive who has successfully broken the cycle of fear also knows that management tactics based on fear aren't effective. For example, I remember the hellfire-and-brimstone sermons that were often masterfully delivered by traveling evangelists in the southern churches where I was raised. They were real scorchers—you couldn't possibly sit and listen without feeling some guilt. The descriptions of eternal hell and damnation were vivid. The screaming pain of knowing that we could have lived our lives differently, we were told, would haunt us forever if we didn't change our ungodly ways. Separated from all loved ones, we would be condemned to a tortuous fire that had no relief.

What is most interesting about those fear-based sermons, as I now look back upon them, is that they usually sparked a temporary revival in the church. People started attending services that hadn't come to church in years. Many of the "backsliden" church members reformed their ways and returned with fervor to the faith.

But it was always short-lived. After a few weeks, often with church services continuing through the weekdays, the excitement began to fade and the revival would wane. The vivid images of life in hell failed to motivate the congregation to *stay* on the straight and narrow. As everyday life outside the church continued, the members found themselves slowly slipping back into the well-worn ruts of their ordinary and not so sanctified habits.

As has been proven in psychological research, using fear-based tactics on others does not create lasting motivation. It spurs immediate action, but its effect soon fades. Lasting motivation that persists through changing circumstances comes from the fulfillment of intrinsic needs, not scare tactics. The sermons that did build lasting attendance in the church of my childhood weren't fearful; rather, they offered hope and peace of mind. These spoke to the daily demands of everyday life.

The same principle operates in organizations. Fear tactics—threatening "corrective action," loss of wages, a demotion—are effective for short bursts of activity, but don't bring about lasting change. In addition, they create a great deal of lingering resentment, lose their power with repeated use, and contribute to the burnout of otherwise effective employees. Ultimately, the threats must become more aggressive to retain their power to motivate.

On the other hand, appealing to employees' innate needs for satisfaction, recognition, and acceptance creates powerful and persistent motivations. With these motivators, there is no need for ever increasing campaigns and programs to boost the morale of resentful employees.

KITA (KICK IN THE ASS)

In 1968, Frederick Herzberg published an article titled "One More Time: How Do You Motivate Employees?" in the *Harvard Business Review*.[1] In the more than thirty years since then, that article has sold well over a million copies in reprint form. Herzberg made a simple but elegant point in this article, which is as relevant today as it was back then. Management actions that function as a "kick in the ass," or KITA, are not effective motivators. Why? They are demeaning, produce resentment, and eventually diminish an employee's performance.

Herzberg made the observation that KITA, despite the negative consequences, is very popular with American managers. In a 1987 update to the original article, he notes that "we seem to be losing ground to KITA." A tyrannical bottom-line mentality that values shareholder dividends and management salaries over the welfare of workers is causing a steady rise in KITA practices. Produce the numbers, or you're out of here. Make your goal, and you get the corner office.

There is a fundamental difference between the manager who uses KITA and the fearless executive. The KITA manager is essentially a pedagogue—a demanding schoolmaster—who insists that employees make the grade and pass the test. He looks down on the employee and is constantly assessing her progress. When the employee falls short, punishments are meted out; and when she succeeds, prizes are awarded.

The fearless executive treats the employee as an equal and supports her in her quest for accomplishment. There is no need for the employee to fight for her position, because she is already a valued member of the team. Instead, the manager functions as an assistant or a coach when one is needed. His attitude from the very beginning communicates trust and respect, and a belief in the employee's ability to do the job. The employee is not struggling to make the grade, but to be her very best. The esteem of the fearless executive supports her in this quest.

The fearless executive has no need for the manipulative tactics of KITA. She is confident in her own talents and has no need of subverting others to make herself look good. She is certain that her talents will produce all the "shine" she needs to succeed.

No Place for Aggression

Fearlessness isn't the same as ruthless aggression. Fearlessness comes from a confidence in one's own abilities, while aggression comes from fear and anger. Consider what has happened to the aggressive leadership practiced in one company, Columbia HCA.

In 1987, Rick Scott, a young Dallas attorney, pooled $125,000 in savings with another financier to buy two El Paso, Texas, hospitals. Those two hospitals formed the beginning of Columbia Hospital Corporation, which quickly amassed more than 90 hospitals. By 1993, the hospital chain had grown into a $20 billion company with 342 hospitals. In 1997, Columbia attempted a merger with Tenet Healthcare, which would have created the largest health-care company in the United States.

The phenomenal growth of Columbia can be attributed to the art of the deal. Scott, a talented and freewheeling deal maker, negotiated the purchase of thirty health-care concerns and approached some eighty more in 1997 alone. No doubt his success lay in Columbia's ability to spot hospitals on the brink of a financial crisis and to arrive on the scene as a "white knight," saving the day. As Martin Brotman, head of California Pacific Medical Center said, "They're very good at smelling blood in the water. . . . They get a whiff and get in there with their buckets of money so fast."[2]

The hallmark of the Columbia deal is iron-fisted aggressiveness. One tactic, as reported by Bloomberg News, includes warning community hospitals that Columbia will build a competing facility nearby if they don't sell out. Other tactics include negotiating secretly with hospital administrators, and then asking the hospital board of directors to approve a deal without knowing the purchase price and terms. More than a few hospital administrators who arranged these secret deals are now employed by Columbia.

Of great concern to many communities is Columbia's unwillingness to continue charity and indigent care services that were offered by the hospitals before they were acquired. Institutions that were founded and funded on the basis of emergency and indigent care are no longer providing those much needed services.

Columbia has also been aggressive in its advertising. Among other tactics, Columbia rents billboards near the entrance to many of their competitors, advertising the local Columbia hospital. For example, across the street from the main entrance to Baptist Hospital, its chief competitor in Oklahoma City, Columbia rented a large billboard advertising the competing Columbia facilities in the area.

What has this behavior earned Columbia? Aggressive opposition. A few of the defensive actions being taken against the company include the following. In Cookeville, Tennessee, nearly one thousand residents turned out to encircle their nonprofit hospital and "hug" the institution. The hospital was not sold. In Rhode Island, the legislature imposed a limit on the number of hospitals that for-profit companies could buy after Columbia expressed strong interest in local hospitals. California Attorney General Dan Lundgren blocked a proposed deal between Columbia and San Diego's highly regarded Sharp Hospital, saying it would severely limit the hospital's ability to continue its charitable and trust obligations. Attorneys general in Michigan and Ohio have also raised objections to Columbia's deals. In Florida, the University of Miami Medical Center voted down a proposed lease of the hospital after it considered Columbia's reputation.

And these are the least of Columbia's troubles. It seems the aggressiveness of company leadership has spread down through corporate culture and spawned other combative if not questionable practices. Most notably, the FBI requested and obtained fifty-one search warrants to enter Columbia offices and search for evidence of fraudulent Medicare billing. By the end of 1999 three executives were indicted, with the FBI promising more to come.

At the time of this writing, Rick Scott had been forced to resign as CEO. The executive who replaced Scott as head of Columbia, Dr. Paul Frist, repeatedly stated that the company planned to take a less aggressive stance in the future. In the words of *Time* magazine, "In the end, Scott's hubris may have cost him his empire."[3]

Unbridled aggression has brought much of Columbia's own tactics back home to roost. The company will be dealing with the drag of its own reputation for many years to come. According to Linda Miller, president of the Volunteer Trustees of Not-For-Profit Hospitals, "Columbia did manage to wear a target on its chest" because of the "aggressive style of Rick Scott." With its own actions, Columbia created an unfavorable reaction.

A NATURAL HONESTY

Another distinct sign of the fearless executive is hard-driving honesty. Executives who don't fear the truth have no need to lie. Honesty creates the solid business relationships that make executives so successful.

When suppliers can trust what they are told by the company as absolute truth, they are willing to do more than they would otherwise. Employees who feel that the company is being straight with them respond with honesty and trustworthiness. Customers come to respect a brand name that they know will deliver exactly what is promised. Shareholders hold a stock longer when they know that management is being completely honest in its projections, even when profitability is disappointing.

If honesty in the modern corporation is dead, it is buried on Madison Avenue. The "art of selling" has permeated the corporation, often forcing the truth to take a backseat to the dressed-up, turbocharged marketing pitch. These days, no one dares introduce a new program within the organization without seriously considering the "education" of users. They "sell" it to upper management, "test" market it on focus groups, and, if things should go bad, employ damage control, which can include such questionable activities as discrediting and silencing critics.

The problem with this marketing approach to corporate relationships is not that it necessarily produces blatant lies but that it often distorts the truth beyond recognition. Managers may promise virtually anything they think the corporate decision makers want to hear if the managers think it will advance their careers.

This varnishing and stretching of the truth creates enormous problems for the organization and, eventually, for the manager who consistently indulges in the practice. Taken to extremes, the organization may make major decisions based on programs and products that exist only on overhead transparencies and glossy handouts—little more than unrealistic promises made in the heat of the moment. Good intentions disintegrate under the weight of reality, and in time those unfulfilled expectations come back to indict the manager who set them.

Where does dishonesty in the organization start? It starts with you and me, every day. Each day we are dishonest in many ways. For example, we arrive at a 7:00 A.M. meeting, after a Herculean effort to arrange for child-care to accommodate the unusually early hour. We smile and act as if the early hour were no problem for us.

In the meeting, we support proposals that we really haven't thought through, but because the boss supports them, we jump on the bandwagon. Poised and intent, we act as if we are really listening to a boring presentation when, in reality, we aren't hearing a word of it. Then, when the human resources representative starts talking about the importance of office safety, we nod our head in agreement, all the while thinking about what a complete waste of time this is.

The point is organizational civility requires us to engage in a certain amount of dishonesty. If we were completely honest all of the time, social order would be virtually impossible. So we simply hide or glaze over the truth with something that is more acceptable, allowing the organization to run smoothly.

The trouble starts when the line between these "socially

acceptable lies" and the truth becomes blurred. We no longer recognize what is true and what isn't. We become more and more willing to embellish facts, making them more appetizing to our audience. We put a spin on reality that makes it more acceptable to the organization. By slowly building one embellished fact upon another, we move on an arc that ends far from the actual truth.

Not only does this dishonesty cause the organization to make decisions based on "bad data," it also erodes trust among members of the organization. Without trust, the essential ingredient of all relationships, the connections that hold the organization together begin to break down.

One of the principles of modern physics, which has contributed heavily to current organizational theory, states that matter is nothing but relationships. That's the glue of an organization—relationships. Without honesty, there is no trust, and consequently only weak relationships can develop. Ultimately, this translates into a dramatically weakened organization.

On the other hand, genuine honesty only strengthens the organizational infrastructure. It builds tempered relationships that can bear enormous stress during times of crisis. This honesty is not always easy or pleasant, but it is effective in creating the best possible organization.

FEARLESS MATCHMAKING

Fearless executives, no longer threatened by up-and-coming, talented employees, become matchmakers of a sort; they work hard to match an employee with a job that will utilize and accentuate the employee's talents. They officiate, as it were, the marriage between the work and the worker. They support the pair, allowing the relationship to grow and flourish. At times, they are the marriage counselor, helping the struggling employee to find her passion within the work.

Much of the "magic" in great leadership lies in matchmaking. Of all the many tasks given an executive, the creation of a dynamic romance between an eager employee and a job is one of the more thrilling. It is part analysis, part hard work, and much intuition. Matchmaking is an art that resides in the eye and heart of every great executive.

Many of the problems of the modern corporation can be traced back to the decline of the matchmaker. Employees are thrown into jobs for which they have little or no interest. Managers of these employees have forsaken their role as matchmaker and have, instead, taken on the yoke of the taskmaster. They parcel out work to employees as if they were interchangeable robots, as if the dreams and desires of employees were of no value to the organization.

Dreams and desires of employees are of solid monetary value to the corporation, for they are the only energy the corporation has. Without dreams and desires, there is little reason to push harder. There is no point in improving. Innovation withers.

Sadly, through years of constant reorganizations, little attention has been paid to the ongoing tasks of the executive matchmaker, creating instead marriages of convenience. These temporary arrangements between employees and jobs are passionless betrothals that are doomed to do little more than maintain the status quo. They are arrangements that provide the employee with a paycheck and the job with an incumbent. While these arrangements maintain social order and "keep up appearances," they deprive both the employee and the organization of more fulfilling and productive possibilities. In time, employees are hardened and embittered by years of loveless work, and they become dead weights that, with collective force, drag the organization down, slowing its pace and paralyzing its ability to change.

Matchmaking is one of the most important roles of any manager. The knack for spotting talent and matching it to the right job is a skill that is paramount in shaping the high-potential organization. Those who would aspire to be great executives must also aspire to the role of matchmaker and counselor. After all, what made you a great executive was matching your talent with your work, and what will ensure your future success is the success of those you manage.

ON BECOMING FEARLESS

In closing, I'd like to tell you about a time in my early life that I learned the power of passion and talent. As you read through my story, remind yourself of those passionate people who crossed your path and changed your life and career forever.

Mrs. Borders was the best teacher I ever had. I'll never forget the humid spring afternoon she did the impossible: She taught a rambunctious ninth-grade class about the soulful essence of literature. It was a lesson I have never forgotten.

The windows that lined the south end of the classroom were all open and the smell of cut grass filled the classroom as the tractor droned on, cutting the grass of the distant running track. It was the kind of sap-rising afternoon that steals the attention of teenagers and fills their minds with wild daydreams and anticipation. This was the day that Mrs. Borders read to us Edgar Allen Poe's "Annabel Lee."

As she started, "It was many and many a year ago . . . ," her voice gracefully sailed over the words, dipping and lunging with rhythm and emotion. She carried us away with her love of the story as she seemed to read a poem that we, for a moment, believed was her own. As she haltingly delivered to us the tragic end of Poe's beautiful maiden, I noticed the tears sparkling in her eyes and slipping down her rounded cheeks. Once finished, silence reigned over a mesmerized classroom. She gently closed the book, folded her hands, looked down in silence, and then said to us, "This is what great literature is all about. Never forget it."

And I haven't.

On another occasion, I remember a new student teacher arriving in Mrs. Border's classroom. Mrs. Borders walked in her stately manner to the door and extended her hand. "Welcome," she said to the grinning novice, "to the best job you'll ever have." After introducing the new student teacher to the class, she gave her some of the most profound advice I have ever been blessed to overhear: "If the day ever comes that you walk through that door and don't feel a spark of excitement, that should be your last day as a teacher."

Mrs. Borders had found her soul's calling, and she wasn't about to let anyone placed in her care settle for less. Being in the presence of a Mrs. Borders, a person so in love with her job, is an electrifying experience. To describe such a passionate endeavor such as "work" seems to defile it, much like describing a joyous endeavor as a tiresome burden.

So now I must ask: What is it that you yearn to do? What brings you great satisfaction? What do you do well? Why don't you do more of it? What is the fear—the dark adviser—that tells you not to try, that dire circumstances will overtake you should you try? What is the destiny that lies in your talents? Why are you not fulfilling that destiny?

You have everything you need to achieve executive success. When all is said and done you can have an executive career that is successful in the most important measure: your fulfillment. Your career can be significant, and you already have the ability to make it happen. You can choose the path of courage. You can become the fearless executive.

Trust your talents. Follow your passion. Silence the fear.

NOTES

1. Frederick Herzberg, "One More Time: How Do You Motivate Employees?" *Harvard Business Review*, January–February 1968.
2. Ellen Hale, "Selling or Selling Out? How Community Hospitals Are Changing Hands," *Gannett News Service*, October 13, 1996.
3. John Greenwald, *Time*, August 4, 1997.

Index

accepted, desire to be, 52–53
achievement
    of fearlessness, 196–207
    and worth, 45–46
action
    environment for, 176–177
    from fear, 14
    fear of, 173, 176
    infectious character of, 175–176
    and luck, 177
    and taking small steps, 174–175
advantages, 122–123
aggression, 200–202
aging, fear of, 108–114
    and fear of death, 112
    and need to prove competence, 111–112
    in senior executives, 109–111
    steps for overcoming, 113–114
    and willingness to undertake "fresh
        starts," 112–113
Alcoholics Anonymous, 47
Alexandra, Empress, 10
Allied Signal, 169
Amelio, Gilbert F., on leadership, 134
American Express, 193, 194
analysis paralysis, 16–17
Animal Farm (George Orwell), 100–102
appearances, reality vs., 85–87
Apple Computers, 70–73, 140
AT&T, 119
authority, fear of, 100–107
    and belief in authority figures, 103–104
    and desire to please others, 104
    far-reaching effects of, 102
    and self-interest, 103, 105–106
    steps for overcoming, 104–107
authority figures, belief in, 103–104
Avery, Sewell Lee, 37–39

Barach, Michael, 45
Baum, L. Frank, 81, 82
"beginner's luck," 177
beliefs, irrational, *see* irrational beliefs
Bessemer Venture Partners, 45
Biddle, Francis, 39
blaming, 148–149
Bossidy, Lawrence, 169
Branson, Richard, 4

Brotman, Martin, 200
Bryson, John, on future leaders, 173
Buffett, Warren, 4
Bundy, McGeorge, 55
burnout, 146
Burton, Robert, on fear, 9
busyness, 111, 179–180
Byham, William, 119

Callas, Maria, 137
Campbell, Joseph, on mythological heroes,
    190–191
career passages, executive, *see* passage(s),
    executive career
career path, decisions about, 147–148
"carried away," getting, 153
Cartoon Corner, 45
change
    avoidance of, 93–94
    desire to stop, 68–70
    during uneventful times, 154
Chicken Soup for the Soul, 64
Chrysler Corporation, 133
CIO (Congress of Industrial Organiza-
    tions), 38
Columbia HCA, 200–202
communism, 140
competence, need to prove, 111
competitive greed, 70–73
Computer Associates International,
    165–166
Congress of Industrial Organizations
    (CIO), 38
consensus, decision by, 61
consultants, 79, 109–110
Crandall, Arthur, on making mistakes, 43
creativity, 161–162
Crouch, John, 72
cycle of fear, 22, 24–25
    and fear of aging, 113–114
    and fear of authority, 104–107
    and fear of inadequacy, 42–47
    and fear of reality, 85–89
    and fear of rejection, 62–66
    and fear of scarcity, 75–78
    and fear of unknown, 94–99
cynicism, 176

Dayton Hudson, *ix*
de Geus, Arie, on scenario planning, 98–99
death, fear of, 112
decision making
    about career, 147–148
    by consensus, 61
    and fear, 16–18
delegation of weaknesses, 131–132
Deloitte & Touche, 109–110
detail, passion for, 167
Dilbert, 110
Disney, Elias, 91
Disney, Roy, 91, 92
Disney, Walt, 91–93
Domino's Pizza, 159–161
Don't Sweat the Small Stuff, 94
Duran, Beverly, on believing in yourself,
    157

Edison, Thomas, 140
education, and talent, 122–123
Eisner, Michael, on passion and creativity,
    161–162
Ellsberg, Daniel, on Lyndon Johnson's
    Vietnam policy, 54
emotional wounds, 12–14
"The Emperor's New Clothes," 48–52
empire building, 41–42
entry jobs, 185–188
excitement, need for, 162–163
experience, 124

fads, business, 80–81
failure, learning from, 44
Faxon, Brad, 138–139
Fear Susceptibility Inventory, 26–32
fear(s), 4–6
    of action, 173, 176
    of aging, 108–114
    of authority, 100–107
    basic properties of, 12–25
    as breach of trust in self, 17–18
    breaking the cycle of, 25
    of death, 112
    feeling vs. acting upon, 14
    and growth, 19–20
    and ignorance, 18–19
    of imagined catastrophes, 15–17
    of inadequacy, 33–47
    location of, 12–14
    messages of, 9
    opponent process model of, 20–21
    of reality, 79–89
    of recognition, 48–66
    of scarcity, 67–78
    self-perpetuating nature of, 20–25
    as state vs. trait, 10
    and talent, 125
    unavoidability of, 14–15
    of unknown, 90–99
Federal Express, 126
feedback, and fear of rejection, 58–61
finiteness, 75–76
Fiorina, Carly, 148
focusing, 2, 4, 120–121
Ford, Henry, II, 133

Ford Motor Company, 133
fulfillment, 159, 182

Gates, Bill, 4, 165
Gerstner, Lou, 193–194
getting along with others, 181
Glasser, William, 162
goals, and passion, 156–158
Graff, Henry, on Lyndon Johnson's cabi-
    net, 55
Graham, Katharine, 20
greed, competitive, 70–73
Greenspan, Alan, 113, 122–123
groupthink, 61
Grove, Andrew, on fear of rejection, 59–60
growth, and fear, 19–20

happiness, and use of talents, 117–120
hard work, 152
Helms, Richard, 55
Herzberg, Frederick, 199
Hewlett-Packard (HP), *ix*, 93, 95–96, 148
honesty, 202–204
HP, *see* Hewlett-Packard

Iacocca, Lee, 133
IBM, 193, 194
Icahn, Carl, 67
ignorance, and fear, 18–19
imagined catastrophes, fear about, 15–17
inadequacy, fear of, 33–47
    in Sewell Lee Avery, 37–39
    and empire building, 41–42
    and myth of "infallible executive,"
        35–37
    and need to win, 39–40
    in Old Testament, 33–35
    steps for overcoming, 42–47
    and use of "spin," 40–41
    in workaholics, 39
"infallible executive," myth of, 35–37
integrity, and fear of rejection, 56–57
intelligence, talent vs., 123
intelligent risk, 95
interdependence, 63
irrational beliefs
    about aging, 113
    about authority, 104–106
    about inadequacy, 42–46
    about reality, 85–88
    about rejection, 62–64
    about scarcity, 75–77
    about the unknown, 94–97

Jobs, Steve, 71–73
Johnson, John H.
    on energy derived from focusing, 2
    on getting ahead, 95
Johnson, Lyndon B., 53–56, 59
Judeo-Christian tradition, 35, 191

Kennedy, John, 18–19
KITA, 199–200

labels (for problems), 84
learning, rapid, 128–130
Lincoln, Abraham, on speaking up, 176

Lisa computer, 70–73
The Living Company (Arie de Geus), 98–99
loved, desire to be, 52–53
luck
  and action, 177
  and success, 87–88

Macintosh computer, 72–73
matchmaking, 204–205
Mays, J., 175
Mays, William G., on failure, 44
McKinsey and Company, 193
McNamara, Robert, 55
Mercer Management, 67
Microsoft, 165
Miller, Linda, 202
mistakes, making, 43–45
moderate success, 182
Monaghan, Tom, 159–161
Monet, Claude, 140
Montgomery Ward, 37–39
Morris, Robert, 136–137
Moses, 191–192
Moyers, Bill, on Lyndon Johnson's cabinet, 55
Murdock, David, 113
Murray, Terry, on self-confidence, 36

Nicholas II, Emperor, 10
Nixon, Richard, 58–59
No Exit (Jean-Paul Sartre), 90–91
Noyce, Robert N., 156, 168

opponent process model of fear, 20–21
Orwell, George, 100
others
  desire to please, 104
  getting along with, 181
  opinions of, 63–64

pain, avoiding, 88
parents, dreams of, 154–155
passage(s), executive career, 183–207
  achievement of fearlessness as, 196–207
  entry job as, 185–188
  proving ground as, 189–195
passion
  ambivalence about, 2
  as basic need, 162–163
  and blaming, 148–149
  case example of, 159–161
  and creativity, 161–162
  for detail, 167
  finding your, 150–151, 169–170
  and goals, 156–158
  losing touch with, 145–146
  as motive, 2
  myths related to, 151–155
  for power, 164–166
  and premature career decisions, 147–148
  for selling, 167
  for structure, 166
  and success, 158–159
  for teamwork, 167–168
  for troubleshooting, 168–169
  working from, 148
passive aggression, 62

personal best, 122
Pew, Robert, 113
Piersanti, Steve, *xi*
Platt, Lew, 4, 95
Post-it® notes, 174–176
potential, reaching your highest, 1, 120
power, passion for, 164–166

quick fixes, desire for, 80–84
quiet time, 153–154

rapid learning, 128–130
Rasputin, 9–10
Reagan, Ronald, 112–113
reality, fear of, 79–89
  and belief in shortcuts, 84–85
  and desire for quick fixes, 80–84
  and "naming the problem," 84
  overcoming fear of, 85–89
Reeve, Christopher, 13
reigns of terror, 198–199
rejection, fear of, 48–66
  cascading effect of, 56
  and consensus decision making, 61
  and desire to be accepted/loved by others, 52–53
  and distortion of truth, 61–62
  and feedback, 58–61
  integrity vs., 56–57
  in Lyndon B. Johnson, 53–56
  origins of, 57
  and passive aggression, 62
  steps for overcoming, 62–66
  in "The Emperor's New Clothes," 48–52
resistance, 179–182
Reznicek, Bernard W., on talent, hard work and commitment, 1
risk
  and fear, 19–20
  intelligent, 95
RJR Nabisco, 193–194
Rogers, Cathy Schnaubelt, on loving your work, 148
Roosevelt, Franklin D., 38
Rotella, Bob, 138
Rusk, Dean, 55

Samson, 33–35, 37
Sartre, Jean-Paul, 90
satisfaction
  and talent, 127–128
  from wealth, 151–152
scarcity, fear of, 67–78
  and competitive greed, 70–73
  and desire to stop change, 68–70
  personal aspects of, 73–75
  steps for overcoming, 75–78
scenario planning, 98–99
Scott, Rick, 202
Sears, Drs. Robert and Pauline, 123
secrecy, 19
self-confidence, 36, 95
selling, passion for, 167
senior executives, fear of aging in, 109–111
shortcuts, 84–85
Silver, Spencer, 174–176

skills, talents vs., 123–124
Smith, Fred, 126
Soviet Union, 140
"spin," 40–41
Steamboat Willie (film), 92
strengths, and weaknesses, 134–135
stress envy, 112
structure, passion for, 166
"styles," management, 181
success
    best-kept secret of executive, 2
    and luck, 87–88
    moderate, 182
    and passion, 158–159
    and talent, 139
    wealth as measure of, 76–77
Swiss watches, 93

talent(s)
    adapting the job to fit your, 130–132,
      140–141
    and advantages, 122–123
    attractiveness of, 139–140
    danger of operating outside, 135–138
    definition of, 121
    and delegation of weaknesses, 131–132
    discovering your, 125–133
    and experience, 124
    and fear, 125
    happiness derived from using, 117–120
    intelligence vs., 123
    and job, 121–122
    need to focus on, 120–121
    nonuse of, 138–139
    and personal best, 122
    and rapid learning, 128–130
    and satisfaction, 127–128
    skills vs., 123–124
    as strategic advantage, 2
    and success, 139
    and yearnings, 126–127
teamwork, passion for, 167–168
Terman, Louis, 123
3M Corporation, 174–175
tired, being, 180–181

Titanic (film), 16
troubleshooting, passion for, 168–169
trust, fear as breach of, 17–18
truth
    fear of rejection and telling the, 61–62
    and honesty, 202–204
TWA, 67

unknown, fear of, 90–99
    and avoidance of change, 93–94
    in industry, 93
    in movie industry, 91–93
    steps for overcoming, 94–99
U.S. Gypsum, 38, 39

Vietnam War, 54, 58–59
Volkswagen Beetle, 175

Wall, Jim, on hiring older consultants,
    109–110
Wal-Mart, 146–147
Walton, Sam, 146–147
Wang, Charles, 165–166
Ward, A. Montgomery, on business
    growth, 164
Warren Commission, 18–19
Washington, George, 136, 137
weaknesses
    delegating, 131–132
    embracing, 42–43
    and strengths, 134–135
wealth
    as measure of success, 76–77
    satisfaction from, 151–152
Welch, Jack, 4
Wheeler, Earl, 55
win, need to, 39–40
Windsor, Duke and Duchess of, 69
The Wizard of Oz (L. Frank Baum), 81–83,
    197
Woods, Tiger, 137
workaholics, 39
wounds, emotional, 12–14
Wozniac, Steve, 140

yearnings, 126–127